VOLUME 1 MASTERWORKS OF SCIENCE

MASTERWORKS OF
SCIENCE

VOLUME 1

DIGESTS OF

EUCLID: ELEMENTS

ARCHIMEDES: ON FLOATING BODIES, AND
OTHER PROPOSITIONS

COPERNICUS: ON THE REVOLUTIONS OF THE
HEAVENLY SPHERES

NEWTON: PRINCIPIA

EINSTEIN: RELATIVITY

EDITED BY JOHN WARREN KNEDLER, JR.

McGraw-Hill Book Company

New York   •   St. Louis   •   San Francisco   •   London   •   Düsseldorf

Kuala Lumpur   •   Mexico   •   Montreal   •   Panama   •   São Paulo

Sydney   •   Toronto   •   Johannesburg   •   New Delhi   •   Singapore

Masterworks of Science, Volume I

First McGraw-Hill Paperback Edition, 1973

07-040813-0

1 2 3 4 5 6 7 8 9 MU MU 7 9 8 7 6 5 4 3

CONTENTS

ACKNOWLEDGMENTS

THE EDITOR wishes to thank Peter Smith, Publisher, for permission to include our condensation of *Relativity: The Special and General Theory,* by Albert Einstein.

J. W. K., JR.

VOLUME 1 MASTERWORKS OF SCIENCE

THE ELEMENTS

by

EUCLID

CONTENTS

The Elements

Definitions

Postulates

Axioms

EUCLID

fl. 300 B.C.

ONE FACT is known with certainty about the Greek mathematician Euclid: he taught in Alexandria in the time of Ptolemy I and founded a school there. All other biographical details must be prefixed with a "probably." Probably he learned mathematics in Athens, probably from pupils of Plato. Several anecdotes told concerning him come from very early commentators and probably contain reflections of truth. When King Ptolemy asked him if there were no shorter way in geometry than that of the *Elements,* he replied: "There is no royal road to geometry." And when a pupil who had mastered the first proposition in the *Elements* inquired what he would get by learning such things, Euclid called a slave and instructed him to give the pupil threepence, "since he must needs make gain by what he learns."

From such biographical bits a reader may piece together a notion of Euclid as a severe but not humorless teacher, a stern, bold seeker after mathematical truth. But details about his personal and family life, about his appearance and habits, about his non-mathematical occupations and ideas, did not interest his early biographers. To learn something about Euclid, modern students must go straight to the task of studying his writings.

These writings, edited in a definitive edition in eight volumes (Heiberg and Menge, *Euclidis opera omnia,* Leipzig, 1883–1916), include the *Data, On Divisions* (of figures), *Optics, Phaenomena,* and the *Elements.* (At least four other treatises, three of them on higher geometry, have been lost.) All of these discuss problems in geometry. The *Elements* has been the standard textbook in geometry for more than two thousand years—a record unequaled by any other treatise on any subject whatsoever—and surely qualifies therefore as a Masterwork.

The *Elements* is divided into thirteen books. The first six and the last three are devoted to geometry, plane and solid; three others are devoted to arithmetic, and one is devoted to irrationals. It is the first six books which have been the study of generation after generation of schoolboys, with whom Euclid and geometry have become synonymous. But geometry is really much older than Euclid.

Geometry means "earth measurement." In the ancient world the need for earth measurements appeared acutely in Egypt because the annual floods of the Nile made surveying constantly necessary for the re-establishment of boundaries. In Egypt, therefore, a practical, applied geometry developed. It consisted of a number of crude rules for the measurement of various simple geometric figures, for laying out angles, particularly right angles, and so on. The Greeks developed this crude beginning into demonstrative geometry. That is, various mathematicians among the Greeks worked out a series of propositions so logically interrelated that if the proof of one is granted or assumed, later ones, based on it, can be proved logically from the assumptions therein demonstrated.

As early as 500 B.C., Hippocrates of Chios compiled a series of such propositions. Succeeding geometers did the same thing. Euclid analyzed the work of his predecessors, arranged the various propositions in an order of his own, introduced new proofs of some propositions, and thus composed his masterwork, the *Elements*. In the first six books about 170 geometrical propositions are presented and proved. Of these only one is certainly original with Euclid—the proof of the Pythagorean theorem, that in any right-angled triangle the square on the hypotenuse is equal to the sum of the squares on the other two sides. Yet so much needed was Euclid's editorial work that from the time of the first appearance of the *Elements,* all earlier compilations were neglected.

If geometrical propositions be arranged—as Euclid's are— in such an order that each one depends for its proof upon the acceptance of propositions earlier proved, it is evident that, proceeding backwards, one comes to an early proposition, perhaps several of them, which cannot be logical consequences of preceding ones. The logical status of these early propositions rests upon various definitions which must be precedent, and upon various assumptions or postulates or axioms the truth of which must be granted before any logical structure can be erected upon them. The first book of the *Elements* is therefore preceded by a set of definitions and a set of assumptions; and later books have, when it is necessary, similar prefaces.

The definitions seem to modern readers elementary. The axioms seem self-evident to the point that statements of them are needless. That they are thus acceptable to us merely shows how completely our common geometric ideas stem from Euclid. For the postulates in particular, being undemonstrable, can be abandoned, and alternate or contrary postulates set up. Upon these a new geometry can be based. Several modern mathematicians have done exactly this, and from their work— notably Riemann's—comes what is known as non-Euclidean geometry.

The design of any systematic geometer must be to reduce the number of definitions and postulates to a minimum. That is, he will wish to assume as little as possible, and to force the truth of his propositions upon the reader by the might of his logic. Euclid may have originated the definitions and axioms with which his treatise begins. Possibly he rather selected from similar lists prepared by earlier geometers. Of the origin of the definitions with which the following selection begins, nothing is certainly known. Of the axioms, number 12 is acknowledged to be Euclid's.

A proposition consists of various parts. There is first the general statement of the problem or theorem, then the construction—which states the necessary straight lines and circles which must be drawn to assist in the demonstration of the theorem—and last the demonstration itself, closing Q.E.F.— *quod erat faciendum*—"which was to be constructed"—or Q.E.D.—*quod erat demonstrandum*—"which was to be proved."

The portion of the *Elements* which follows is verbatim from the edition of Euclid prepared by Isaac Todhunter in 1862. It includes a number of the definitions and all the postulates and axioms which precede Book I; the first five propositions with their full Euclidean construction and demonstration, of which number 5 is the notorious *pons asinorum,* or bridge of asses, so called because it has ever been an obstacle to schoolboys; and number 47 from the first book, the famous Pythagorean theorem.

THE ELEMENTS

DEFINITIONS

1. A point is that which has no parts, or which has no magnitude.
2. A line is length without breadth.
3. The extremities of a line are points.
4. A straight line is that which lies evenly between its extreme points.
5. A superficies is that which has only length and breadth.
6. The extremities of a superficies are lines.
7. A plane superficies is that in which any two points being taken, the straight line between them lies wholly in that superficies.
8. A plane angle is the inclination of two lines to one another in a plane, which meet together, but are not in the same direction.
9. A plane rectilineal angle is the inclination of two straight lines to one another, which meet together, but are not in the same straight line.

10. When a straight line standing on another straight line makes the adjacent angles equal to one another, each of the angles is called a right angle; and the straight line which stands on the other is called a perpendicular to it.

11. A term or boundary is the extremity of any thing.
12. A figure is that which is enclosed by one or more boundaries.

13. A circle is a plane figure contained by one line, which is called the circumference, and is such that all straight lines drawn from a certain point within the figure to the circumference are equal to one another:

14. And this point is called the centre of the circle.

15. A diameter of a circle is a straight line drawn through the centre, and terminated both ways by the circumference.

[A radius of a circle is a straight line drawn from the centre to the circumference.]

16. Rectilineal figures are those which are contained by straight lines:

17. Trilateral figures, or triangles, by three straight lines:

18. Quadrilateral figures by four straight lines:

19. Multilateral figures, or polygons, by more than four straight lines.

20. Of three-sided figures,
An equilateral triangle is that which has three equal sides:

21. An isosceles triangle is that which has two sides equal:

22. A scalene triangle is that which has three unequal sides:

23. A right-angled triangle is that which has a right angle:

Of four-sided figures,
24. A square is that which has all its sides equal, and all its angles right angles:

25. An oblong is that which has all its angles right angles, but not all its sides equal:

26. A rhombus is that which has all its sides equal, but its angles are not right angles:

27. A rhomboid is that which has its opposite sides equal to one another, but all its sides are not equal, nor its angles right angles:

28. All other four-sided figures besides these are called trapeziums.

29. Parallel straight lines are such as are in the same plane, and which being produced ever so far both ways do not meet.

[Some writers propose to restrict the word *trapezium* to a quadrilateral which has two of its sides parallel; and it would certainly be convenient if this restriction were universally adopted.]

POSTULATES

Let it be granted,

1. That a straight line may be drawn from any one point to any other point:

2. That a terminated straight line may be produced to any length in a straight line:

3. And that a circle may be described from any centre, at any distance from that centre.

AXIOMS

1. Things which are equal to the same thing are equal to one another.
2. If equals be added to equals the wholes are equal.
3. If equals be taken from equals the remainders are equal.
4. If equals be added to unequals the wholes are unequal.
5. If equals be taken from unequals the remainders are unequal.
6. Things which are double of the same thing are equal to one another.
7. Things which are halves of the same thing are equal to one another.
8. Magnitudes which coincide with one another that is, which exactly fill the same space, are equal to one another.
9. The whole is greater than its part.
10. Two straight lines cannot enclose a space.
11. All right angles are equal to one another.
12. If a straight line meet two straight lines, so as to make the two interior angles on the same side of it taken together less than two right angles, these straight lines, being continually produced, shall at length meet on that side on which are the angles which are less than two right angles.

PROPOSITION 1. PROBLEM

To describe an equilateral triangle on a given finite straight line.
Let *AB* be the given straight line: it is required to describe an equilateral triangle on *AB*.

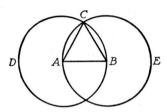

From the centre *A*, at the distance *AB*, describe the circle *BCD*.
[*Postulate* 3.
From the centre *B*, at the distance *BA*, describe the circle *ACE*.   [*Post.* 3.
From the point *C*, at which the circles cut one another, draw the straight lines *CA* and *CB* to the points *A* and *B*.   [*Postulate* 1.
ABC shall be an equilateral triangle.
Because the point *A* is the centre of the circle *BCD*, *AC* is equal to *AB*.   [*Definition* 13.
And because the point *B* is the centre of the circle *ACE*, *BC* is equal to *BA*.   [*Definition* 13.
But it has been shewn that *CA* is equal to *AB*;
therefore *CA* and *CB* are each of them equal to *AB*.
But things which are equal to the same thing are equal to one another.   [*Axiom* 1.
Therefore *CA* is equal to *CB*.
Therefore *CA*, *AB*, *BC* are equal to one another.
Wherefore *the triangle ABC is equilateral*,   [*Definition* 20.
and it is described on the given straight line AB.   Q.E.F.

PROPOSITION 2. PROBLEM

From a given point to draw a straight line equal to a given straight line.
Let *A* be the given point, and *BC* the given straight line: it is required to draw from the point *A* a straight line equal to *BC*.
From the point *A* to *B* draw the straight line *AB*;   [*Postulate* 1.
and on it describe the equilateral triangle *DAB*,   [I. 1.
and produce the straight lines *DA*, *DB* to *E* and *F*.   [*Postulate* 2.
From the centre *B*, at the distance *BC*, describe the circle *CGH*, meeting *DF* at *G*.   [*Postulate* 3.

From the centre *D*, at the distance *DG*, describe the circle *GKL*, meeting
DE at *L*.   [*Postulate* 3.
AL shall be equal to *BC*.

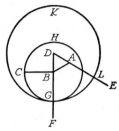

Because the point *B* is the centre of the circle *CGH*, *BC* is equal to
BG.   [*Definition* 13.
And because the point *D* is the centre of the circle *GKL*, *DL* is equal to
DG;   [*Definition* 13.
and *DA*, *DB* parts of them are equal;   [*Definition* 20.
therefore the remainder *AL* is equal to the remainder *BG*.   [*Axiom* 3.
But it has been shewn that *BC* is equal to *BG*;
therefore *AL* and *BC* are each of them equal to *BG*.
But things which are equal to the same thing are equal to one another.
                                                               [*Axiom* 1.

Therefore *AL* is equal to *BC*.
        Wherefore *from the given point A a straight line AL has been drawn
equal to the given straight line BC.*   Q.E.F.

PROPOSITION 3. PROBLEM

*From the greater of two given straight lines to cut off a part equal
to the less.*
        Let *AB* and *C* be the two given straight lines, of which *AB* is the
greater: it is required to cut off from *AB*, the greater, a part equal to *C*
the less.

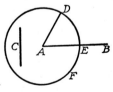

From the point *A* draw the straight line *AD* equal to *C*;   [I. 2.
and from the centre *A*, at the distance *AD*, describe the circle *DEF* meeting *AB* at *E*.   [*Postulate* 3.
AE shall be equal to *C*.

Because the point *A* is the centre of the circle *DEF*, *AE* is equal to *AD*.   [*Definition* 13.
But *C* is equal to *AD*.   [*Construction*.
Therefore *AE* and *C* are each of them equal to *AD*.
Therefore *AE* is equal to *C*.   [*Axiom* 1.
  Wherefore *from AB the greater of two given straight lines a part AE has been cut off equal to C the less*.   Q.E.F.

PROPOSITION 4. THEOREM

If two triangles have two sides of the one equal to two sides of the other, each to each, and have also the angles contained by those sides equal to one another, they shall also have their bases or third sides equal; and the two triangles shall be equal, and their other angles shall be equal, each to each, namely those to which the equal sides are opposite.

Let *ABC*, *DEF* be two triangles which have the two sides *AB*, *AC* equal to the two sides *DE*, *DF*, each to each, namely, *AB* to *DE*, and *AC* to *DF*, and the angle *BAC* equal to the angle *EDF*: the base *BC* shall be equal to the base *EF*, and the triangle *ABC* to the triangle *DEF*, and the other angles shall be equal, each to each, to which the equal sides are opposite, namely, the angle *ABC* to the angle *DEF*, and the angle *ACB* to the angle *DFE*.

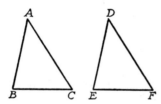

For if the triangle *ABC* be applied to the triangle *DEF*, so that the point *A* may be on the point *D*, and the straight line *AB* on the straight line *DE*, the point *B* will coincide with the point *E*, because *AB* is equal to *DE*.   [*Hypothesis*.
And, *AB* coinciding with *DE*, *AC* will fall on *DF*, because the angle *BAC* is equal to the angle *EDF*.   [*Hypothesis*.
Therefore also the point *C* will coincide with the point *F*, because *AC* is equal to *DF*.   [*Hypothesis*.

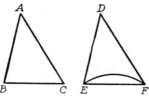

But the point B was shewn to coincide with the point E, therefore the base BC will coincide with the base EF;

because, B coinciding with E and C with F, if the base BC does not coincide with the base EF, two straight lines will enclose a space; which is impossible.   [*Axiom* 10.

Therefore the base BC coincides with the base EF, and is equal to it.

[*Axiom* 8.

Therefore the whole triangle ABC coincides with the whole triangle DEF, and is equal to it.   [*Axiom* 8.

And the other angles of the one coincide with the other angles of the other, and are equal to them, namely, the angle ABC to the angle DEF, and the angle ACB to the angle DFE.

Wherefore, *if two triangles* &c.   Q.E.D.

PROPOSITION 5.   THEOREM

The angles at the base of an isosceles triangle are equal to one another; and if the equal sides be produced the angles on the other side of the base shall be equal to one another.

Let ABC be an isosceles triangle, having the side AB equal to the side AC, and let the straight lines AB, AC be produced to D and E: the angle ABC shall be equal to the angle ACB, and the angle CBD to the angle BCE.

In BD take any point F,

and from AE the greater cut off AG equal to AF the less,   [I. 3.

and join FC, GB.

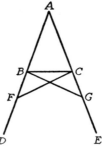

Because AF is equal to AG,   [*Construction.*

and AB to AC,   [*Hypothesis.*

the two sides FA, AC are equal to the two sides GA, AB, each to each; and they contain the angle FAG common to the two triangles AFC, AGB; therefore the base FC is equal to the base GB, and the triangle AFC to the triangle AGB, and the remaining angles of the one to the remaining angles of the other, each to each, to which the equal sides are opposite, namely the angle ACF to the angle ABG, and the angle AFC to the angle AGB.   [I. 4.

And because the whole *AF* is equal to the whole *AG*, of which the parts *AB*, *AC* are equal,   [*Hypothesis.*
the remainder *BF* is equal to the remainder *CG*.   [*Axiom 3.*
And *FC* was shewn to be equal to *GB*;
therefore the two sides *BF*, *FC* are equal to the two sides *CG*, *GB*, each to each;
and the angle *BFC* was shewn to be equal to the angle *CGB*; therefore the triangles *BFC*, *CGB* are equal, and their other angles are equal, each to each, to which the equal sides are opposite, namely the angle *FBC* to the angle *GCB*, and the angle *BCF* to the angle *CBG*.   [I. 4.

And since it has been shewn that the whole angle *ABG* is equal to the whole angle *ACF*,
and that the parts of these, the angles *CBG*, *BCF* are also equal;
therefore the remaining angle *ABC* is equal to the remaining angle *ACB*, which are the angles at the base of the triangle *ABC*.   [*Axiom 3.*

And it has also been shewn that the angle *FBC* is equal to the angle *GCB*, which are the angles on the other side of the base.

Wherefore, *the angles* &c. Q.E.D.

Corollary. Hence every equilateral triangle is also equiangular.

PROPOSITION 47. THEOREM

In any right-angled triangle, the square which is described on the side subtending the right angle is equal to the squares described on the sides which contain the right angle.

Let *ABC* be a right-angled triangle, having the right angle *BAC*: the square described on the side *BC* shall be equal to the squares described on the sides *BA*, *AC*.

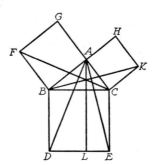

On *BC* describe the square *BDEC*, and on *BA*, *AC* describe the squares *GB*, *HC*;
through *A* draw *AL* parallel to *BD* or *CE*;
and join *AD*, *FC*.

Then, because the angle *BAC* is a right angle,   [*Hypothesis.*
and that the angle *BAG* is also a right angle,   [*Definition 24.*

the two straight lines *AC*, *AG*, on the opposite sides of *AB*, make with it at the point *A* the adjacent angles equal to two right angles;
therefore *CA* is in the same straight line with *AG*.
For the same reason, *AB* and *AH* are in the same straight line.

Now the angle *DBC* is equal to the angle *FBA*, for each of them is a right angle.   [*Axiom* 11.
Add to each the angle *ABC*.
Therefore the whole angle *DBA* is equal to the whole angle *FBC*.
[*Axiom* 2.
And because the two sides *AB*, *BD* are equal to the two sides *FB*, *BC*, each to each;   [*Definition* 24.
and the angle *DBA* is equal to the angle *FBC*;
therefore the triangle *ABD* is equal to the triangle *FBC*.   [I. 4.

Now the parallelogram *BL* is double of the triangle *ABD*, because they are on the same base *BD*, and between the same parallels *BD*, *AL*.
[I. 41.
And the square *GB* is double of the triangle *FBC*, because they are on the same base *FB*, and between the same parallels *FB*, *GC*.   [I. 41.
But the doubles of equals are equal to one another.   [*Axiom* 6.
Therefore the parallelogram *BL* is equal to the square *GB*.

In the same manner, by joining *AE*, *BK*, it can be shewn, that the parallelogram *CL* is equal to the square *CH*. Therefore the whole square *BDEC* is equal to the two squares *GB*, *HC*.   [*Axiom* 2.
And the square *BDEC* is described on *BC*, and the squares *GB*, *HC* on *BA*, *AC*.
Therefore the square described on the side *BC* is equal to the squares described on the sides *BA*, *AC*.

Wherefore, *in any right-angled triangle* &c. Q.E.D.

ON FLOATING BODIES, AND OTHER PROPOSITIONS

by

ARCHIMEDES

CONTENTS

On Floating Bodies, and Other Propositions

ARCHIMEDES

287–212 B.C.

ARCHIMEDES was born too late to study under Euclid. But when, as a young man, he went to Alexandria to study, his instructors in mathematics there were students and successors of Euclid. Ever afterward he considered himself a geometer. Physicists remember him for his investigations into the behavior of floating bodies and for his studies of the lever. Historians mention his invention of military engines used by his kinsman, Hieron of Syracuse, to stave off the besieging Romans. He himself regarded his practical inventions and his mechanical inquiries as the "diversions of geometry at play." Plutarch reports of him that he "possessed so lofty a spirit, so profound a soul, and such a wealth of scientific knowledge that . . . he would not consent to leave behind him any written work on such subjects, but, regarding as ignoble and sordid the business of mechanics and every sort of art which is directed to practical utility, he placed his whole ambition in those speculations in the beauty and subtlety of which there is no admixture of the common needs of life." It is recorded that he wished to have placed on his tomb a representation of a cylinder circumscribing a sphere within it, together with an inscription giving the ratio 3/2 which the cylinder's volume bears to the sphere's. Apparently he considered the discovery of this mathematical relationship to be his great claim upon posterity's regard.

The episodes of Archimedes' life cannot clearly be read in the conflicting accounts which give any information about him. After the years of study in Egypt he returned to the Greek city of Syracuse in Sicily, his birthplace, there to spend his days in studying geometry save when, at the command of the king, he did occasionally apply himself to mechanics. He was killed when the Romans finally took Syracuse and sacked it. A picturesque version of his death says that while he was working over an intricate geometrical diagram, a Roman soldier came too close. Archimedes ordered: "Stand aside, fellow, from my diagram!" Immediately the conquering soldier, in a rage, killed him. If the story is not true, it at least underlines the notion elsewhere derived that Archimedes died, as he had lived, in the midst of mathematical speculation.

Unlike Euclid, Archimedes was not a compiler of geometrical propositions and an editor of the work of others. Rather, taking the work of others as completed, he embarked on new inquiries based on what they had accomplished. He remarks in one of his letters that, in connection with the attempts of earlier geometers to square the circle, he noticed that no one had tried to square a parabolic segment. Taking the problem for his own, he eventually solved it. In the preface to one of his works he reviews the theorems of a predecessor, Eudoxus, about the pyramid, cone, and cylinder, and approves them. Then he offers, as supplements to the work of Eudoxus, his own greater discoveries about the relative surfaces and volumes of cylinders and spheres.

The works of Archimedes—so far as they remain to us— include two books on the sphere and cylinder, two on plane equilibriums, two on floating bodies, one each on spirals, on conoids and spheroids, on the parabola, and on the measurement of the circle. There is a work called *Method* in which he tells, in the form of a letter to a friend, how he generally conceived of a theorem by means of mechanics and then proceeded to a rigorous geometrical proof of it. And another work, *The Sand Reckoner,* is a curiosity of mathematics, invaluable to our knowledge of Greek astronomy by reason of the materials it uses, and fascinating because it reveals the versatility and ingenuity of Archimedes. It begins with the observation that the sands have been called innumerable chiefly because sufficiently large numbers do not exist to record their numbers. Then, assuming that the whole universe is compact of sand, Archimedes shows that a system of numbers can readily be formed to express the total. His method amounts to our modern one of expressing large numbers as powers of ten. But the Greeks used letters and words, not numerals, to express numbers. Archimedes had, therefore, to invent a method of "orders" and "periods" so that he could write the higher powers of numbers. He thus succeeds in expressing in a few words any number up to that which in modern notation would be written as 1 followed by 80,000 billion ciphers.

Various references, many of them Arabian, indicate that Archimedes composed other works than those listed. Though he did live a long span, it is hard to understand where, in a lifetime so productive of mathematical masterpieces, he found time and energy to perfect also the mechanical devices, methods, and principles for which the non-mathematical world reveres him. Historians of science call him the greatest mathematician of antiquity, perhaps the greatest mathematical genius of all time. They admire him for his application of the principle of exhaustion to geometrical measurement, a practice in which he anticipates the calculus of Leibnitz and Newton. Less specialized historians remember his work on levers, his invention of war machines for hurling missiles, his experiments to discover whether the king's crown were pure gold or a mixture of gold and silver—an experiment in which he evolved a method for measuring specific gravity. Every schoolboy knows the story, possibly true, of how, in his excitement over solving a problem which he had been pondering while he bathed, he ran naked through the streets shouting "Eureka"—that is, "I've got it."

Of the mechanical appliances which Archimedes invented, there is no record in his own words. Of his work on levers, floating bodies, and so on, there remains a series of theorems and demonstrations which constantly indicate that he had learned his method of rigorous mathematical proof from Euclid's *Elements*. In fact, so precisely does he apply the Euclidean method that frequently a reader does not understand as he reads an initial theorem whither it will lead. For example, the second theorem on Floating Bodies proves that the surface of any fluid at rest is the surface of a sphere the center of which is the center of the earth. Then in logical order follow four theorems devoted to the behavior of solids placed in liquids. Finally, at Proposition 7, occurs the statement now known to us as Archimedes' principle—that a solid immersed in a fluid is buoyed up by a force equal to the weight of the fluid displaced. Plutarch remarks that it is not possible "to find in geometry more difficult and troublesome questions, or more simple and more lucid explanations." The lucidity and simplicity, all editors agree, is a real miracle of workmanship.

In geometry, Archimedes built upon the work of his predecessors. In mechanics, and particularly in hydrostatics, he was a wholly original workman. He had the ability to see a problem in all its difficulties, to plan an attack upon it, and —so far as records show—always to conquer the obstacles in the way of a solution. Yet he was honest and modest enough to make a great point in one of his prefaces of confessing that certain views he had previously held were in error. He thus presents to posterity the picture of the perfect scientist—one

ON FLOATING BODIES, AND OTHER PROPOSITIONS

ON THE SPHERE AND CYLINDER

"Archimedes to Dositheus greeting.

On a former occasion I sent you the investigations which I had up to that time completed, including the proofs, showing that any segment bounded by a straight line and a section of a right-angled cone [a parabola] is four-thirds of the triangle which has the same base with the segment and equal height. Since then certain theorems not hitherto demonstrated (ἀνελέγκτων) have occurred to me, and I have worked out the proofs of them. They are these: first, that the surface of any sphere is four times its greatest circle (τοῦ μεγίστου κύκλου); next, that the surface of any segment of a sphere is equal to a circle whose radius (ἡ ἐκ τοῦ κέντρου) is equal to the straight line drawn from the vertex (κορυφή) of the segment to the circumference of the circle which is the base of the segment; and, further, that any cylinder having its base equal to the greatest circle of those in the sphere, and height equal to the diameter of the sphere, is itself [*i.e.* in content] half as large again as the sphere, and its surface also [including its bases] is half as large again as the surface of the sphere. Now these properties were all along naturally inherent in the figures referred to (αὐτῇ τῇ φύσει προυπῆρχεν περὶ τὰ εἰρημένα σχήματα), but remained unknown to those who were before my time engaged in the study of geometry. Having, however, now discovered that the properties are true of these figures, I cannot feel any hesitation in setting them side by side both with my former investigations and with those of the theorems of Eudoxus on solids which are held to be most irrefragably established, namely, that any pyramid is one third part of the prism which has the same base with the pyramid and equal height, and that any cone is one third part of the cylinder which has the same base with the cone and equal height. For, though these properties also were naturally inherent in the figures all along, yet they were in fact unknown to all the many able geometers who lived before Eudoxus, and had not been observed by any one. Now, however, it will be open to those who possess the requisite ability to examine these discoveries of mine. They ought to have been published while Conon was still alive, for I should conceive that he would best have been able to grasp them and to pronounce upon them the appropriate verdict; but, as I judge it well to communicate them to those who are conversant with mathematics, I send them to you with the proofs written out, which it will be open to mathematicians to examine. Farewell.

I first set out the assumptions which I have used for the proofs of my proposition.

Assumptions

1. Of all lines which have the same extremities the straight line is the least.

2. Of other lines in a plane and having the same extremities, [any two] such are unequal whenever both are concave in the same direction and one of them is either wholly included between the other and the straight line which has the same extremities with it, or is partly included by, and is partly common with, the other; and that [line] which is included is the lesser [of the two].

3. Similarly, of surfaces which have the same extremities, if those extremities are in a plane, the plane is the least [in area].

4. Of other surfaces with the same extremities, the extremities being in a plane, [any two] such are unequal whenever both are concave in the same direction and one surface is either wholly included between the other and the plane which has the same extremities with it, or is partly included by, and partly common with, the other; and that [surface] which is included is the lesser [of the two in area].

5. Further, of unequal lines, unequal surfaces, and unequal solids, the greater exceeds the less by such a magnitude as, when added to itself, can be made to exceed any assigned magnitude among those which are comparable with [it and with] one another.

These things being premised, *if a polygon be inscribed in a circle, it is plain that the perimeter of the inscribed polygon is less than the circumference of the circle;* for each of the sides of the polygon is less than that part of the circumference of the circle which is cut off by it.

Proposition

If a polygon be circumscribed about a circle, the perimeter of the circumscribed polygon is greater than the perimeter of the circle.

Let any two adjacent sides, meeting in *A*, touch the circle at *P*, *Q* respectively.

Then [*Assumptions, 2*]
$$PA + AQ > (\text{arc } PQ).$$

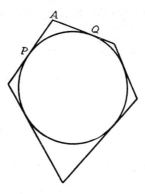

A similar inequality holds for each angle of the polygon; and, by addition, the required result follows.

MEASUREMENT OF A CIRCLE

Proposition 1

The area of any circle is equal to a right-angled triangle in which one of the sides about the right angle is equal to the radius, and the other to the circumference, of the circle.

Proposition 2

The area of a circle is to the square on its diameter as 11 to 14.

Proposition 3

The ratio of the circumference of any circle to its diameter is less than $3\frac{1}{7}$ but greater than $3\frac{10}{71}$.

I. Let AB be the diameter of any circle, O its centre, AC the tangent at A; and let the angle AOC be one-third of a right angle.

Then $OA:AC > 265:153$ .... (1),

and $OC:CA = 306:153$ .... (2).

First, draw OD bisecting the angle AOC and meeting AC in D.

Now $CO:OA = CD:DA$,   [Eucl. VI. 3]

so that $[CO+OA:OA = CA:DA$, or]

$CO+OA:CA = OA:AD$.

Therefore by (1) and (2)

$$OA:AD > 571:153 \dots\dots\dots\dots\dots (3).$$

Hence
$$OD^2:AD^2 = (OA^2 + AD^2):AD^2$$
$$> (571^2 + 153^2):153^2$$
$$> 349450:23409,$$

so that
$$OD:DA > 591\tfrac{1}{8}:153 \dots\dots\dots\dots (4).$$

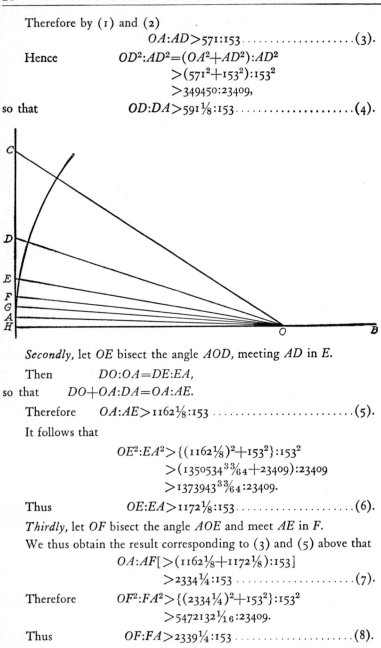

Secondly, let OE bisect the angle AOD, meeting AD in E.

Then
$$DO:OA = DE:EA,$$
so that
$$DO + OA:DA = OA:AE.$$

Therefore
$$OA:AE > 1162\tfrac{1}{8}:153 \dots\dots\dots\dots (5).$$

It follows that
$$OE^2:EA^2 > \{(1162\tfrac{1}{8})^2 + 153^2\}:153^2$$
$$> (1350534\tfrac{33}{64} + 23409):23409$$
$$> 1373943\tfrac{33}{64}:23409.$$

Thus
$$OE:EA > 1172\tfrac{1}{8}:153 \dots\dots\dots\dots (6).$$

Thirdly, let OF bisect the angle AOE and meet AE in F.

We thus obtain the result corresponding to (3) and (5) above that
$$OA:AF[> (1162\tfrac{1}{8} + 1172\tfrac{1}{8}):153]$$
$$> 2334\tfrac{1}{4}:153 \dots\dots\dots\dots (7).$$

Therefore
$$OF^2:FA^2 > \{(2334\tfrac{1}{4})^2 + 153^2\}:153^2$$
$$> 5472132\tfrac{1}{16}:23409.$$

Thus
$$OF:FA > 2339\tfrac{1}{4}:153 \dots\dots\dots\dots (8).$$

Fourthly, let OG bisect the angle AOF, meeting AF in G.

We have then

$$OA:AG > (2334\tfrac{1}{4} + 2339\tfrac{1}{4}):153, \text{ by means of (7) and (8)}$$
$$> 4673\tfrac{1}{2}:153.$$

Now the angle AOC, which is one-third of a right angle, has been bisected four times, and it follows that

$$\angle AOG = \tfrac{1}{48} \text{ (a right angle).}$$

Make the angle AOH on the other side of OA equal to the angle AOG, and let GA produced meet OH in H.

Then $\qquad \angle GOH = \tfrac{1}{24}$ (a right angle).

Thus GH is one side of a regular polygon of 96 sides circumscribed to the given circle.

And, since $\qquad OA:AG > 4673\tfrac{1}{2}:153,$

while $\qquad AB = 2OA, \quad GH = 2AG,$

it follows that

$$AB:(\text{perimeter of polygon of 96 sides}) [> 4673\tfrac{1}{2}:153 \times 96]$$
$$> 4673\tfrac{1}{2}:14688.$$

But

$$\frac{14688}{4673\tfrac{1}{2}} = 3 + \frac{667\tfrac{1}{2}}{4673\tfrac{1}{2}}$$
$$< 3 + \frac{667\tfrac{1}{2}}{4672\tfrac{1}{2}}$$
$$< 3\tfrac{1}{7}.$$

Therefore the circumference of the circle (being less than the perimeter of the polygon) is *a fortiori* less than $3\tfrac{1}{7}$ times the diameter AB.

II. Next let AB be the diameter of a circle, and let AC, meeting the circle in C, make the angle CAB equal to one-third of a right angle. Join BC.

Then $\qquad AC:CB < 1351:780.$

First, let AD bisect the angle BAC and meet BC in d and the circle in D. Join BD.

Then $\qquad \angle BAD = \angle dAC$
$$= \angle dBD,$$

and the angles at D, C are both right angles.

It follows that the triangles ADB, $[ACd]$, BDd are similar.

Therefore $\qquad AD:DB = BD:Dd$
$$= AB:Bd \qquad \text{[Eucl. VI. 3]}$$
$$= AB + AC:Bd + Cd$$
$$= AB + AC:BC$$

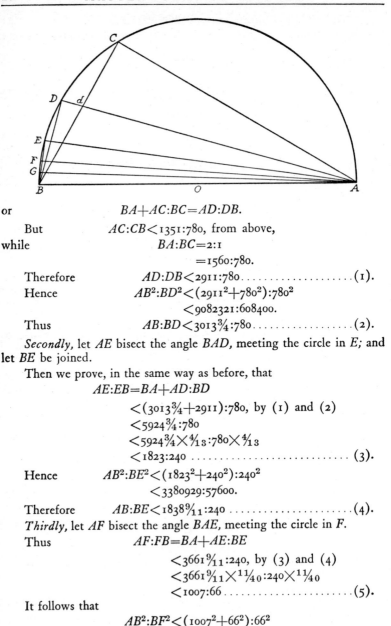

or $\qquad BA+AC:BC=AD:DB.$

But $\qquad AC:CB<1351:780$, from above,

while $\qquad BA:BC=2:1$

$$=1560:780.$$

Therefore $\qquad AD:DB<2911:780\dots\dots\dots\dots\dots\dots(1).$

Hence $\qquad AB^2:BD^2<(2911^2+780^2):780^2$

$$<9082321:608400.$$

Thus $\qquad AB:BD<3013\tfrac{3}{4}:780\dots\dots\dots\dots\dots(2).$

Secondly, let AE bisect the angle $BAD,$ meeting the circle in $E;$ and let BE be joined.

Then we prove, in the same way as before, that

$$AE:EB=BA+AD:BD$$

$$<(3013\tfrac{3}{4}+2911):780, \text{ by (1) and (2)}$$

$$<5924\tfrac{3}{4}:780$$

$$<5924\tfrac{3}{4}\times\tfrac{4}{13}:780\times\tfrac{4}{13}$$

$$<1823:240\dots\dots\dots\dots\dots\dots\dots\dots(3).$$

Hence $\qquad AB^2:BE^2<(1823^2+240^2):240^2$

$$<3380929:57600.$$

Therefore $\qquad AB:BE<1838\tfrac{9}{11}:240\dots\dots\dots\dots\dots\dots(4).$

Thirdly, let AF bisect the angle $BAE,$ meeting the circle in $F.$

Thus $\qquad AF:FB=BA+AE:BE$

$$<3661\tfrac{9}{11}:240, \text{ by (3) and (4)}$$

$$<3661\tfrac{9}{11}\times\tfrac{11}{40}:240\times\tfrac{11}{40}$$

$$<1007:66\dots\dots\dots\dots\dots\dots\dots(5).$$

It follows that

$$AB^2:BF^2<(1007^2+66^2):66^2$$

$$<1018405:4356.$$

Therefore $\qquad AB:BF < 1009\frac{1}{6}:66$ . . . .(6).

Fourthly, let the angle BAF be bisected by AG meeting the circle in G.

Then $\qquad AG:GB = BA + AF:BF$

$\qquad\qquad\qquad\qquad < 2016\frac{1}{6}:66$, by (5) and (6).

And $\qquad AB^2:BG^2 < \{(2016\frac{1}{6})^2 + 66^2\}:66^2$

$\qquad\qquad\qquad\qquad < 4069284\frac{1}{36}:4356$.

Therefore $\qquad AB:BG \quad < 2017\frac{1}{4}:66$,

whence $\qquad\qquad BG:AB > 66:2017\frac{1}{4}$ . . . .(7).

Now the angle BAG which is the result of the fourth bisection of the angle BAC, or of one-third of a right angle, is equal to one-forty-eighth of a right angle.

Thus the angle subtended by BG at the centre is

$\qquad\qquad\frac{1}{24}$ (a right angle).

Therefore BG is a side of a regular inscribed polygon of 96 sides.

It follows from (7) that

$\qquad$ (perimeter of polygon)$:AB[> 96 \times 66:2017\frac{1}{4}]$

$\qquad\qquad\qquad\qquad\qquad\qquad > 6336:2017\frac{1}{4}$.

And $\qquad\qquad \dfrac{6336}{2017\frac{1}{4}} > 3\frac{10}{71}$.

Much more then is the circumference of the circle greater than $3\frac{10}{71}$ times the diameter.

Thus the ratio of the circumference to the diameter

$\qquad\qquad < 3\frac{1}{7}$ but $> 3\frac{10}{71}$.

ON THE EQUILIBRIUM OF PLANES
OR
THE CENTRES OF GRAVITY OF PLANES

I POSTULATE the following:

1. Equal weights at equal distances are in equilibrium, and equal weights at unequal distances are not in equilibrium but incline towards the weight which is at the greater distance.

2. If, when weights at certain distances are in equilibrium, something be added to one of the weights, they are not in equilibrium but incline towards that weight to which the addition was made.

3. Similarly, if anything be taken away from one of the weights, they are not in equilibrium but incline towards the weight from which nothing was taken.

4. When equal and similar plane figures coincide if applied to one another, their centres of gravity similarly coincide.

5. In figures which are unequal but similar the centres of gravity will be similarly situated. By points similarly situated in relation to similar figures I mean points such that, if straight lines be drawn from them to the equal angles, they make equal angles with the corresponding sides.

6. If magnitudes at certain distances be in equilibrium, (other) magnitudes equal to them will also be in equilibrium at the same distances.

7. In any figure whose perimeter is concave in (one and) the same direction the centre of gravity must be within the figure.

Proposition 1

Weights which balance at equal distances are equal.

For, if they are unequal, take away from the greater the difference between the two. The remainders will then not balance [*Post.* 3]; which is absurd.

Therefore the weights cannot be unequal.

Proposition 2

Unequal weights at equal distances will not balance but will incline towards the greater weight.

For take away from the greater the difference between the two. The equal remainders will therefore balance [*Post.* 1]. Hence, if we add the difference again, the weights will not balance but incline towards the greater [*Post.* 2].

Proposition 3

Unequal weights will balance at unequal distances, the greater weight being at the lesser distance.

Let A, B be two unequal weights (of which A is the greater) balancing about C at distances AC, BC respectively.

Then shall AC be less than BC. For, if not, take away from A the weight $(A-B)$. The remainders will then incline towards B [*Post.* 3]. But

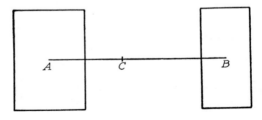

this is impossible, for (1) if $AC=CB$, the equal remainders will balance, or (2) if $AC>CB$, they will incline towards A at the greater distance [*Post.* 1].

Hence $AC<CB$.

Conversely, if the weights balance, and $AC<CB$, then $A>B$.

Proposition 4

If two equal weights have not the same centre of gravity, the centre of gravity of both taken together is at the middle point of the line joining their centres of gravity.

Proposition 5

If three equal magnitudes have their centres of gravity on a straight line at equal distances, the centre of gravity of the system will coincide with that of the middle magnitude.

Cor. 1. *The same is true of any odd number of magnitudes if those which are at equal distances from the middle one are equal, while the distances between their centres of gravity are equal.*

Cor. 2. *If there be an even number of magnitudes with their centres of gravity situated at equal distances on one straight line, and if the two middle ones be equal, while those which are equidistant from them (on each side) are equal respectively, the centre of gravity of the system is the middle point of the line joining the centres of gravity of the two middle ones.*

Proposition 6

Two magnitudes balance at distances reciprocally proportional to the magnitudes.

I. Suppose the magnitudes A, B to be commensurable, and the points A, B to be their centres of gravity. Let DE be a straight line so divided at C that

$$A:B=DC:CE.$$

We have then to prove that, if A be placed at E and B at D, C is the centre of gravity of the two taken together.

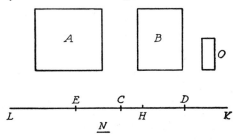

Since A, B are commensurable, so are DC, CE. Let N be a common measure of DC, CE. Make DH, DK each equal to CE, and EL (on CE produced) equal to CD. Then $EH=CD$, since $DH=CE$. Therefore LH is bisected at E, as HK is bisected at D.

Thus LH, HK must each contain N an even number of times.

Take a magnitude O such that O is contained as many times in A as N is contained in LH, whence

$$A:O=LH:N.$$

But
$$B:A=CE:DC$$
$$=HK:LH.$$

Hence, *ex aequali*, $B:O=HK:N$, or O is contained in B as many times as N is contained in HK.

Thus O is a common measure of A, B.

Divide LH, HK into parts each equal to N, and A, B into parts each equal to O. The parts of A will therefore be equal in number to those of LH, and the parts of B equal in number to those of HK. Place one of the parts of A at the middle point of each of the parts N of LH, and one of the parts of B at the middle point of each of the parts N of HK.

Then the centre of gravity of the parts of A placed at equal distances on LH will be at E, the middle point of LH [*Prop. 5, Cor. 2*], and the centre of gravity of the parts of B placed at equal distances along HK will be at D, the middle point of HK.

Thus we may suppose A itself applied at E, and B itself applied at D.

But the system formed by the parts O of A and B together is a system of equal magnitudes even in number and placed at equal distances along LK. And, since $LE=CD$, and $EC=DK$, $LC=CK$, so that C is the middle point of LK. Therefore C is the centre of gravity of the system ranged along LK.

Therefore A acting at E and B acting at D balance about the point C.

ON FLOATING BODIES

Postulate

"Let it be supposed that a fluid is of such a character that, its parts lying evenly and being continuous, that part which is thrust the less is driven along by that which is thrust the more; and that each of its parts is thrust by the fluid which is above it in a perpendicular direction if the fluid be sunk in anything and compressed by anything else."

Proposition 1

If a surface be cut by a plane always passing through a certain point, and if the section be always a circumference of a circle whose centre is the aforesaid point, the surface is that of a sphere.

For, if not, there will be some two lines drawn from the point to the surface which are not equal.

Suppose *O* to be the fixed point, and *A, B* to be two points on the surface such that *OA, OB* are unequal. Let the surface be cut by a plane passing through *OA, OB.* Then the section is, by hypothesis, a circle whose centre is *O.*

Thus *OA=OB;* which is contrary to the assumption. Therefore the surface cannot but be a sphere.

Proposition 2

The surface of any fluid at rest is the surface of a sphere whose centre is the same as that of the earth.

Suppose the surface of the fluid cut by a plane through *O,* the centre of the earth, in the curve *ABCD.*

ABCD shall be the circumference of a circle.

For, if not, some of the lines drawn from *O* to the curve will be un-equal. Take one of them, *OB,* such that *OB* is greater than some of the lines from *O* to the curve and less than others. Draw a circle with *OB* as radius. Let it be *EBF,* which will therefore fall partly within and partly without the surface of the fluid.

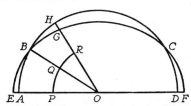

Draw *OGH* making with *OB* an angle equal to the angle *EOB,* and meeting the surface in *H* and the circle in *G.* Draw also in the plane an arc of a circle *PQR* with centre *O* and within the fluid.

Then the parts of the fluid along *PQR* are uniform and continuous, and the part *PQ* is compressed by the part between it and *AB,* while the part *QR* is compressed by the part between *QR* and *BH.* Therefore the parts along *PQ, QR* will be unequally compressed, and the part which is compressed the less will be set in motion by that which is compressed the more.

Therefore there will not be rest; which is contrary to the hypothesis.

Hence the section of the surface will be the circumference of a circle whose centre is *O;* and so will all other sections by planes through *O.*

Therefore the surface is that of a sphere with centre *O.*

Proposition 3

Of solids those which, size for size, are of equal weight with a fluid will, if let down into the fluid, be immersed so that they do not project above the surface but do not sink lower.

If possible, let a certain solid *EFHG* of equal weight, volume for volume, with the fluid remain immersed in it so that part of it, *EBCF*, projects above the surface.

Draw through *O*, the centre of the earth, and through the solid a plane cutting the surface of the fluid in the circle *ABCD*.

Conceive a pyramid with vertex *O* and base a parallelogram at the surface of the fluid, such that it includes the immersed portion of the solid. Let this pyramid be cut by the plane of *ABCD* in *OL, OM*. Also let a sphere within the fluid and below *GH* be described with centre *O*, and let the plane of *ABCD* cut this sphere in *PQR*.

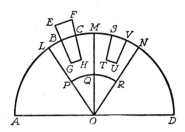

Conceive also another pyramid in the fluid with vertex *O*, continuous with the former pyramid and equal and similar to it. Let the pyramid so described be cut in *OM, ON* by the plane of *ABCD*.

Lastly, let *STUV* be a part of the fluid within the second pyramid equal and similar to the part *BGHC* of the solid, and let *SV* be at the surface of the fluid.

Then the pressures on *PQ, QR* are unequal, that on *PQ* being the greater. Hence the part at *QR* will be set in motion by that at *PQ*, and the fluid will not be at rest; which is contrary to the hypothesis.

Therefore the solid will not stand out above the surface.

Nor will it sink further, because all the parts of the fluid will be under the same pressure.

Proposition 4

A solid lighter than a fluid will, if immersed in it, not be completely submerged, but part of it will project above the surface.

In this case, after the manner of the previous proposition, we assume the solid, if possible, to be completely submerged and the fluid to be at rest in that position, and we conceive (1) a pyramid with its vertex at *O*, the centre of the earth, including the solid, (2) another pyramid continuous with the former and equal and similar to it, with the same vertex *O*, (3) a portion of the fluid within this latter pyramid equal to the immersed solid in the other pyramid, (4) a sphere with centre *O* whose surface is below the immersed solid and the part of the fluid in the second pyramid corresponding thereto. We suppose a plane to be drawn through the centre O cutting the surface of the fluid in the circle ABC, the solid in S, the first pyramid in OA, OB, the second pyramid in OB, OC, the portion of the fluid in the second pyramid in K, and the inner sphere in PQR.

Then the pressures on the parts of the fluid at PQ, QR are unequal, since S is lighter than K. Hence there will not be rest; which is contrary to the hypothesis.

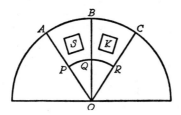

Therefore the solid S cannot, in a condition of rest, be completely submerged.

Proposition 5

Any solid lighter than a fluid will, if placed in the fluid, be so far immersed that the weight of the solid will be equal to the weight of the fluid displaced.

For let the solid be $EGHF$, and let $BGHC$ be the portion of it immersed when the fluid is at rest. As in Prop. 3, conceive a pyramid with vertex O including the solid, and another pyramid with the same vertex continuous with the former and equal and similar to it. Suppose a portion of the fluid $STUV$ at the base of the second pyramid to be equal and similar to the immersed portion of the solid; and let the construction be the same as in Prop. 3.

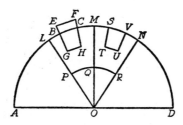

Then, since the pressure on the parts of the fluid at PQ, QR must be equal in order that the fluid may be at rest, it follows that the weight of the portion $STUV$ of the fluid must be equal to the weight of the solid $EGHF$. And the former is equal to the weight of the fluid displaced by the immersed portion of the solid $BGHC$.

Proposition 6

If a solid lighter than a fluid be forcibly immersed in it, the solid will be driven upwards by a force equal to the difference between its weight and the weight of the fluid displaced.

For let A be completely immersed in the fluid, and let G represent the weight of A, and $(G+H)$ the weight of an equal volume of the fluid. Take a solid D, whose weight is H, and add it to A. Then the weight of $(A+D)$ is less than that of an equal volume of the fluid; and, if $(A+D)$ is immersed in the fluid, it will project so that its weight will be equal to the weight of the fluid displaced. But its weight is $(G+H)$.

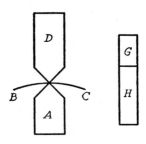

Therefore the weight of the fluid displaced is $(G+H)$, and hence the volume of the fluid displaced is the volume of the solid A. There will accordingly be rest with A immersed and D projecting.

Thus the weight of D balances the upward force exerted by the fluid on A, and therefore the latter force is equal to H, which is the difference between the weight of A and the weight of the fluid which A displaces.

Proposition 7

A solid heavier than a fluid will, if placed in it, descend to the bottom of the fluid, and the solid will, when weighed in the fluid, be lighter than its true weight by the weight of the fluid displaced.

(1) The first part of the proposition is obvious, since the part of the fluid under the solid will be under greater pressure, and therefore the other parts will give way until the solid reaches the bottom.

(2) Let A be a solid heavier than the same volume of the fluid, and let $(G+H)$ represent its weight, while G represents the weight of the same volume of the fluid.

Take a solid B lighter than the same volume of the fluid, and such that the weight of B is G, while the weight of the same volume of the fluid is $(G+H)$.

Let A and B be now combined into one solid and immersed. Then, since $(A+B)$ will be of the same weight as the same volume of fluid, both weights being equal to $(G+H)+G$, it follows that $(A+B)$ will remain stationary in the fluid.

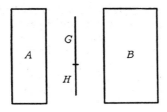

Therefore the force which causes A by itself to sink must be equal to the upward force exerted by the fluid on B by itself. This latter is equal to the difference between $(G+H)$ and G [*Prop.* 6]. Hence A is depressed by a force equal to H, i.e. its weight in the fluid is H, or the difference between $(G+H)$ and G.

ON THE REVOLUTIONS OF
THE HEAVENLY SPHERES

by

NIKOLAUS COPERNICUS

CONTENTS

On the Revolutions of the Heavenly Spheres

NIKOLAUS COPERNICUS

1473-1543

NIKOLAUS COPERNICUS was born in Thorn, in East Prussia, in
1473, the son of a prosperous copper dealer who had married
the daughter of a well-to-do merchant and landowner of that
city. An orphan at ten, he came into the care of his mother's
brother, a rising churchman named Lucas Watzelrode. When
he was nineteen his uncle, now Bishop of Varmia, sent him
to the University of Cracow; a few years later this uncle had
him appointed a canon of Frauenberg cathedral. Thenceforth
Copernicus held always a church office or two; he never ex-
perienced poverty.

At Cracow, Copernicus studied mathematics and astronomy, the use of astronomical instruments, and Aristotle. He
was in Italy, apparently for the second time, in 1498, and he
seems to have gone there to study medicine. He stayed for
three years. During this time, probably, he learned Greek
and developed a taste for humanistic studies. Certainly he
studied astronomy at Bologna, and certainly he lectured on
mathematics in Rome in 1500. At one time he registered at
Bologna as a student of canon law. Subsequently he went to
Padua to study medicine, then to Ferrara to study law, then
back to Padua to study medicine again. In 1503 he returned to
Varmia to live in close association with his uncle for almost
a decade. A trained physician, he served as his uncle's secre-
tary and companion, supervised the diet of the whole elabo-
rately organized episcopal household, bought medical books
for the bishop's library—many of which he annotated—and
cared for the health of the bishop. He was constantly active
in administrative matters as the agent of his uncle or of the
cathedral chapter, constantly in contact in the great cities of
East Prussia and Poland with powerful church and secular
lords. Yet he found time for other activities. He translated
the *Epistles of Simocatta*—a second-rate bit of late Greek

literature—into Latin and published his translation in 1509. It was the first original print of a Greek author in Poland. In the same year he observed a lunar eclipse, one of a large number on which during his long life he made extended notes. More important, he proceeded far enough with his theorizings and speculations to plan his book *De Revolutionibus Orbium Caelestium* (On the Revolutions of the Heavenly Spheres). Though thirty years lapsed before his book was printed, he may already have completed a draft of it when, at forty, he removed from Varmia to Frauenberg. He lived in Frauenberg almost continuously for the next thirty years, until his death in 1543.

During these long years, affairs of the church, of the cathedral chapter, of the secular world, intruded upon the scholar. In 1514 the Pope invited him to Rome to assist in the revision of the calendar. He refused, long afterward explaining that he could not accept because he had not then the accurate knowledge about the courses of the sun and moon which the revisionary task demanded. From 1515 to 1521 he was the administrator of Allenstein and Mehlsack, two tiny provinces in Ermland, and, after a war between the King of Poland and the Prussian Order—during which he defended the castle of Allenstein against the Prussians—he became administrator of all Ermland. In 1519, by invitation, he drew up a memorandum on the need and the means for stabilizing and improving the currency. This he presented to the Diets of Poland, Lithuania, and Prussia several times between 1519 and 1527. Unfortunately, though his ideas were sound, they were not adopted.

Meantime, the greatest tumult of the times, the revolt of Luther from the Church, apparently left Copernicus in remote Ermland quite unperturbed and untouched. A physician of some fame, an astronomer recognized in his own time, an able administrator in public affairs, an architect, a diplomat, a map maker, a warrior, a painter, an economist; indeed a man of almost universal abilities, he was yet a churchman but no theologian. While the storms of controversy roared over Europe, echoing even in Varmia, he continued quietly, persistently, to study the stars from his observatory higher than the cathedral roof in Frauenberg, to collect the data with which to support his theories, and to write and revise the book which eventually overthrew the accepted hypotheses of medieval astronomy.

The astronomical ideas of the Middle Ages all derived from Ptolemy, a second-century Alexandrian. He had left to his successors not only an admirable body of observations and computations, but also five hypotheses: (1) The World is a sphere and revolves as a sphere; (2) The Earth is also a sphere; (3) The Earth is the center of the World; (4) In size, the Earth compared to the World is a mere point; (5) The Earth is motionless. No one had seriously doubted Ptolemy for fifteen hundred years; nor had anyone questioned his views, inherited from the Greek Hipparchus (160–125 B.C), that the planetary motions followed an intricate system of epicycles and eccentrics.

Copernicus particularly queried the fifth hypothesis. Others had done the same: Macrobius, John Scotus Erigena, Averroes, Maimonides, Nicolas of Cusa. But none had carried his queries very far. Copernicus convinced himself that this hypothesis was wholly untenable; then he discovered that number three similarly lacked validity.

In 1514, in a brief work called *Commentariolus,* Copernicus summed up his ideas in seven hypotheses: (1) There is no one center of all the celestial spheres; (2) The center of the Earth, though the center of gravity, is not the center of the World; (3) The planetary spheres revolve round the Sun as their center; (4) The distance of the Earth from the Sun is incommensurable with the dimensions of the firmament; (5) The Earth daily rotates on its axis; (6) The Earth performs more than one motion; (7) The motions of the Earth explain the apparent motions of the heavenly bodies. These propositions sharply modify those of Ptolemy. They are the essential propositions of the *De Revolutionibus.*

For full fifteen years after the composition of the brief *Commentariolus,* Copernicus busied himself in collecting data to substantiate his propositions. He came to believe that the older observations of astronomers were too inaccurate to be dependable, and he substituted for them his own more careful—though still faulty—observations and computations. Probably he constantly revised his book. When in 1539 a young Lutheran scholar from Wittenberg, Rheticus, sought out the famous astronomer in distant Frauenberg, the great work was apparently complete. Rheticus studied it enthusiastically, gave an account of it in a long formal letter to one of his scientific friends (printed as *Narratio Prima* in 1540), and two years later persuaded Copernicus to let him have the whole work printed. The first copy came into the old man's hands on the very day of his death in 1543.

Copernicus had originally planned his work in eight books; later he replanned it in six, of which the first is here translated. It presents the propositions of the *Commentariolus* together with the reasons, astronomical and geometrical, for accepting them. Book II is devoted to spherical astronomy; Book III, to the length of the year and the orbit of the earth;

Book IV, to the moon and its eclipses; Books V and VI, to the planetary motions. The work did not immediately win readers. Twenty years passed before there was a second printing (Basel, 1566), and another fifty before there was a third (1617). Even today it is not available in English. Yet in this long-neglected book Copernicus, almost singlehanded, overthrew the old geocentric theory and established the current heliocentric. Some of his "proofs" are now outmoded, chiefly because Copernicus had to rely upon observations and measurements made with the crudest of instruments. Some of his hypotheses later generations of astronomers have refused, notably the one concerning that motion of the earth which, according to him, explains the precession of the equinoxes. Nevertheless, this book, the lifework of one of the world's great men, is one of the world's greatest.

ON THE REVOLUTIONS OF THE HEAVENLY SPHERES

I. *That the World is Spherical*

FIRST, it must be recognized that the world is spherical. For the spherical is the form of all forms most perfect, having need of no articulation; and the spherical is the form of greatest volumetric capacity, best able to contain and circumscribe all else; and all the separated parts of the world—I mean the sun, the moon, and the stars—are observed to have spherical form; and all things tend to limit themselves under this form—as appears in drops of water and other liquids—whenever of themselves they tend to limit themselves. So no one may doubt that the spherical is the form of the world, the divine body.

II. *That the Earth also is Spherical*

SIMILARLY, the earth is spherical, all its sides resting upon its center. Of course, its perfect sphericity is not immediately seen because of the great height of the mountains and the great depth of the valleys. But these scarcely modify the total rotundity of the earth. Its sphericity is manifest. Indeed, for those who, from any part of the earth, journey towards the north, the pole of diurnal revolution little by little rises and the opposite pole declines, and many stars in the northern region seem never to set, whereas others in the southern regions seem never to rise. Thus Italy never sees Canopus, which is visible in Egypt. And Italy sees the last star of Fluvius, which our country, in a colder zone, knows naught of. Contrarily, for those who journey southward, these constellations rise whereas others, high for us, set. Nevertheless, the inclination of the poles has everywhere the same relation to any portion of the earth—which could not be true if the figure were not spherical. Hence it is clear that the earth is itself limited by poles and is consequently spherical. We may add that dwellers in the East do not see the eclipses of the sun and moon which chance to occur during the night, and that those of the West do not see those occurring by day; those between see these phenomena, some earlier and some later.

That the seas take a spherical form is perceived by navigators. For when land is still not discernible from a vessel's deck, it is from the masthead. And if, when a ship sails from land, a torch be fastened from the masthead, it appears to watchers on the land to go downward little by little until it entirely disappears, like a heavenly body setting. Yet it is certain that water, because of its fluidity, tends downward and does not rise above its container more than its convexity permits. That is why the land is so much the higher, why it rises from the ocean.

III. How the Land and Sea Form but One Globe

THE OCEAN which surrounds the land, pouring its waters every way, fills therewith the deepest depths. There is necessarily, therefore, less water in total than land—granted that both, because of their weight, tend toward the center; otherwise, the waters would cover the land. But for the safety of living creatures, the waters leave free some portions of land such as the numerous islands which are found here and there. As to the continent itself and the whole terrestrial world, is it not merely an island larger than the others?

It is unnecessary to heed those peripatetics who have affirmed that the quantity of water must be ten times that of the land because, as is notorious in the transmutation of elements, one part of land in liquefaction produces ten parts of water. Accepting that idea, they say that the land emerges just to a certain point because, possessing interior cavities, it is not in equilibrium with respect to gravity, and that the center of gravity is different from the center of volume. These men deceive themselves through their ignorance of geometry. They do not understand that even if there were seven times as much water as land, and if any part of the land remained dry, the land would have to withdraw wholly from the center of gravity, yielding place to the water as if it were the heavier element. For spheres are among themselves in the ratio of the cubes of their diameters. If, then, to seven parts of water the land were an eighth, its diameter could not be greater than the distance from the center to the circumference of the water. It is then still less possible that there should be ten times as much water as land. And that there is no difference between the center of gravity of the earth and its center of volume is proved by the fact that the convexity of the land which rises above the waters is not swollen in one smooth abscess; if it were, it would have thrust back the waters wholly and would not, in any manner, be subject to the inroads of interior seas and deep gulfs. Further, the greater the distance from the shore, the greater would be the ocean depths; and sailors departing from land would never encounter an island or a rock or any kind of land.

Now it is well known that between the Egyptian Sea and the Arabian Gulf, almost at the middle of the terrestrial world, the distance is scarcely fifteen stadii. Yet Ptolemy taught that the habitable earth extends to the median circle; beyond that, he indicates unexplored land where moderns have identified Cathay and other vast areas reaching even to 60° of longitude. Thus the habitable land stretches through a greater longitude than is left for the ocean. And if thereto be added the islands discovered in our time under the Spanish and Portuguese princes, and especially all America —thus named by the ship's captain who discovered it—which from its dimensions (so far ill-known) appears to be a second continent, and numerous other islands hitherto unknown, one would not be greatly astonished to learn that there are antipodes and antichthones.

Indeed, geometric reasons force us to believe that America occupies a position diametrically opposite Gangean India. Hence, I think it clear that the land and the water alike tend toward a common center of gravity which is no other than the center of volume of the land, because it is the heavier. It is clear that the partly open portions of the land are filled with water, and that consequently, in comparison to the land, there is not much water even though, at the surface, there appears to be more water than land.

The land together with the water which encompasses it necessarily has the figure which its shadow reveals. Now, during eclipse, the shadow of the earth projected on the moon has the circumference of a perfect circle. In conclusion, then, the earth is not flat, even though Empedocles and Anaximenes thought so; nor is it drum-shaped, as Leucippus thought; nor is it boat-shaped, as Heraclitus thought; nor is it hollowed out in some other form, as Democritus believed; nor is it cylindrical, as Anaximander taught; no more is it infinitely extended downward, growing larger towards its base, as Xenophanes thought; but, as the philosophers thought, it is perfectly spherical.

IV. That the Movement of the Heavenly Bodies is Uniform, Perpetual, and Circular or Composed of Circular Movements

WE SHALL NOW remind ourselves that the motion of the heavenly bodies is circular. Indeed, for a sphere, the appropriate motion is rotation: by that very act, while it moves uniformly in itself, it expresses its form— that of the simplest of bodies in which can be distinguished neither beginning nor end, nor distinction between the one and the other.

Now because there are many spheres, there are varying motions. The most observable of these is the daily revolution which the Greeks called *nychthemeron,* that is, "the space of one day and one night." In that time, the whole of creation except the earth—so they believed—is borne from the east to the west. This motion has been accepted as the common measure for all other motions: we measure time itself usually by number of days. Then we see also other revolutions—some of which are retrograde, that is, going from west to east—notably those of the sun, the moon, and the five planets.

Thus the sun gives us the year and the moon the month, common divisions of time; similarly, each of the five planets travels its own proper course. These motions, however, differ very strongly. First, they are not based on the same poles as the first revolution, but follow the slant of the zodiacal circle (the ecliptic). Then, in their individual circuits, they do not move in uniform fashion. The sun and the moon are discovered to be moving at one time more slowly, at another more rapidly. As for the five wandering stars, we see them sometimes even retrograding, and actually halting between their forward and backward motions. And though the sun ever travels along its route, these five wander in diverse fashions, now towards the south, now towards the north. This is, indeed, the reason for calling them wandering stars (planets). Further, sometimes they approach near to the earth—when they are said to be at the perigee —and at other times they proceed far from the earth—when they are said to be at the apogee. Nevertheless, it must be acknowledged that their paths are circular or composed of circles, for they execute their unequal motions in conformity with a certain law, and repeat the same motions periodically—a phenomenon impossible if their paths were not circular. Only the circle can bring back the past, as, for example, the sun by its motion composed of circular motions brings again to us the inequality of days and nights and of the four seasons.

Several different motions are recognized, for the heavenly bodies can not possibly be moved in an unequal fashion by a single sphere. Indeed, such inequality could occur only through the inconstancy of the moving power, which might conceivably arise from an external or an internal cause or by a modification in the revolving body. Now, since the intellect recoils with horror from these two suppositions, and since it would be unworthy to suppose such a thing in a creation constituted in the best way, it must be admitted that the equal movement of these bodies appears to us unequal either because the various spheres have not the same poles or because the earth is not the center of the circles round which they move. For us who from the earth view the movements of the heavenly bodies, they appear to be larger when they are near us than when they are more distant—an effect explained in optics. Thus the equal movements of the spheres may appear unequal motions in equal times to us, viewing them from different distances. This is the reason that I believe it first of all necessary for us to examine attentively the relation of the earth to the sky, so that, though we desire to study the highest things, we shall not be ignorant of those near at hand, and shall not, by similar error, attribute to heavenly bodies that which appertains to the earth.

V. Is a Circular Movement Suitable to the Earth?

It has been already demonstrated that the earth has the form of a globe, and I think it needful now to examine whether it follows a motion like to its form, and what is the place which it occupies in the universe. Without these bits of knowledge, it will not be possible to explain certain of the phenomena of the heavens. Certainly it is ordinarily so agreed among authors that the earth is at rest at the center of the world that they think it unreasonable and even ridiculous to maintain the contrary. If, however, we examine the question with great attention, it will emerge as not wholly solved, and not beneath inquiry. For all apparent local movement arises either from the motion of the thing observed, or from that of the observer, or from the simultaneous motions—of course unequal—of the two. If two bodies—I have in mind an observer and an object observed—move with equal motion, the motion is not perceived. Now it is from the earth that we observe the motions of the heavenly bodies. If, then, the earth did have some motion, we would observe it in the apparent motion of bodies external to the earth, as if they were swept along at an equal speed, but in an opposite sense; and such, in the first place, is the diurnal revolution. That seems, truly, to carry round the whole world except the earth and objects near it. If it were granted that the heavens have no motion but that the earth rotates from west to east, and if the result of such an assumed motion upon the apparent rising and setting of the sun were seriously examined, it would be found to be precisely as it now appears. And since the heavens embrace and contain all else, and are the common place of all things, it is not immediately clear why motion should be attributed rather to the containing body than to the body contained.

The Pythagoreans Heraclides and Ecphantus thought as much, and so, according to Cicero, did the Syracusan Nicetus. They conceived the earth to be turning at the center of the world. They considered that the stars "set" because the earth moved in front of them, and rose when the earth moved away. But if these views be accepted, there arises another problem no less important: What is the place of the earth? It is agreed by almost everyone that the earth is the center of the world. Yet if anyone were to deny this belief and should grant that the distance from the earth to the center of the world is by no means so great as to be comparable with the dimensions of the sphere of the fixed stars, yet still very great and, from the relations to the spheres of the suns and the other planets, quite obvious; if he should note that the motions of these later bodies appear irregular because they are controlled with relation to another center than the center of the earth; he might perhaps be able to offer an explanation not superficially absurd of the apparent irregularity in the motions of the heavenly bodies. For example: as the wandering stars are observed now nearer to the earth, now farther away, it necessarily follows that the earth is not the center of their circular paths. And it is not clear whether it is the earth which varies its distance from them or they which approach to and retreat from the earth.

It would be scarcely surprising if someone were to attribute to the earth another motion besides the diurnal revolution. Indeed, Philolaus the Pythagorean, a remarkable mathematician, believed, they say, that the earth really moves circularly and at the same time executes several other motions. He considered the earth itself merely one of the stars. It was to see him that Plato did not hesitate to travel to Italy, as those record who have narrated the life of Plato.

On the other hand, a number of philosophers have convinced themselves by geometric arguments that the earth is the center of the world. Indeed, only if it occupies the central position—being like a point in comparison to the immensity of the heavens—can it be, from that fact, motionless. For when the whole universe turns, its center remains still, and those things move slowest which are nearest to the center.

VI. Concerning the Immensity of the Heavens Compared to the Dimensions of the Earth

THAT the size of the earth, though huge, is yet not commensurable with that of the sky can be comprehended from what follows. The limiting circle (thus the Greek term *horizon* is interpreted) cuts the whole celes-

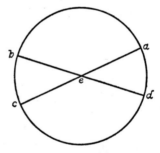

tial sphere into two halves, and it could not were the earth's size great compared to that of the sky ·or to its distance from the center of the world. As is well known, the circle which cuts a sphere into two halves is the greatest circle of the sphere which can be circumscribed upon the sphere's center. Let the circle *a b c d* be the horizon and let *e* be the earth from which we view the horizon, and itself the central point of the horizon which separates the visible from the non-visible stars. Now if, by means of a theodolite, a zodiacal chart, and a level placed at *e,* the beginning of Cancer is identified rising at *c,* at the same instant the beginning of Capricorn will be setting at *a.* But since the points *e, a,* and *c* are on a straight line running across the theodolite, clearly this line is the diameter of the zodiacal circle; for six signs of the zodiac circumscribe the visible stars, and the line center *c* is also the center of the horizon. Now, when a revolution has occurred and the beginning of Capricorn rises at *b,* then the beginning of Cancer is setting at *d.* Then *b e d* is a straight line and is a diameter of the zodiacal circle. But it has already been shown that *a e c* is similarly the diameter of the same circle. Clearly, the center of the circle is at the intersection of these two diameters. Thus, then, the horizon always cuts the circle of the zodiac, which is itself the greatest possible circle of the sphere. And as, on a sphere, any circle which bisects a great circle is itself a great circle, it follows that the horizon is itself a great circle and that its center is the center of the ecliptic. Hence it is obvious that though the line passing across the earth's surface is different from the one passing through its center, yet because of the immensity of their lengths compared to the dimensions of the earth, they are like parallels which seem to form a single line. For because of the very hugeness of their length the distance between them becomes negligible in comparison—as is demonstrated in optics.

Thanks to this reasoning, it seems to be clear that the sky in comparison to the earth is immense, and may almost be considered infinite; and as reckoned by our senses, the earth compared to the sky is as a point to a body, or as the finite to the infinite. Precisely so much is demonstrated.

Now it does not follow from this concept that the earth must be motionless at the center of the world. Indeed, it would be more astonishing that the whole immense world should turn in twenty-four hours than that a little part of it, the earth, should. If it is claimed that a center is motionless and that those things nearest the center move most slowly, this does not prove that the earth remains motionless at the center of the world. It is easily said that the sky turns on unmoving poles, and that that which is nearest the poles is moved the least. Thus the Little Bear appears to us to move much more slowly than the Eagle or Sirius, for, close to the pole, it describes a very small circle; and since all these belong to one sphere, this sphere's motion being less near the pole of the axis does not allow that all its parts shall have motions equal the one to the other. The motion of the whole sweeps along the parts in their respective paths in equal time, but not through equal distances.

Observe now the consequence of the argument that the earth, being a part of the celestial sphere, participating in its nature and its motion, would be little moved because close to the center. It would be moved, it too, existing as a body not the geometric center of the sphere, and would describe in the same time circumferences like the celestial circles, but smaller. Now how false such a motion is, is clearer than day. Were it true, some part of the earth would be ever at high noon, and some other, ever at midnight. At no place would sunrise or sunset ever occur. For the motion of the whole and of the part would be one and inseparable.

Between things separated by a diversity of natures, the relation is wholly different, and such that those which travel a smaller circuit trace it more rapidly than those which travel a longer path. Saturn, for example, the most distant of the planets, moves round its circuit once in thirty years; whereas the moon, which is doubtless of all the planets the closest to the earth, accomplishes its whole journey in a month; and the earth itself turns in the space of a day and a night. Observe that the problem of the diurnal revolution recurs. So does that of the earth's place, not determined by what has preceded. For the earlier demonstration proves only the undefined immensity of the sky as compared to the size of the earth. Yet how far that immensity extends is not at all clear. As with those tiny and indivisible bodies called atoms which, though they are not perceivable by themselves and do not when taken two or several together immediately form a visible body, yet may be multiplied until they join to form finally a great mass; just so it is with the place of the earth: although it is not itself at the center of the world, its distance from the center is not comparable with the immense dimensions of the sphere of the fixed stars.

VII. Why the Ancients Believed that the Earth is Motionless at the Middle of the World as its Center

For a variety of reasons the ancient philosophers asserted that the earth must be the center of the world. They adduced as a principal argument the matter of relative heaviness and lightness. Of the elements, earth is the heaviest; and all heavy objects move towards the earth, plunging towards its interior. Since the earth—towards which heavy things are borne from all sides and perpendicularly to the surface—is round, these heavy things would, if not restrained at the earth's surface, meet at the earth's center. For a straight line perpendicular to a surface tangential to a sphere leads to the sphere's center. Now objects which of themselves move towards a center seek to repose in the center. Surely, then, the earth must be in repose at its center. It receives in itself everything which falls, and must from its weight remain motionless.

These ancients sought to support the same belief by reasoning based on motion and its nature. Aristotle said that the motion of a single, simple body is simple; that of simple motions, one is circular, the other rectilinear; that of rectilinear motions, one is up and the other down. Consequently, every simple motion is directed toward the center—that is, down—or away from the center—that is, up—or around the center—that is, in a circle. To move downward—that is, toward the center—is proper only to the elements earth and water, regarded as the elements which have weight. To move up—that is, away from the center—is proper only to the elements air and fire, regarded as the elements which have lightness. These four elements are limited, therefore, to rectilinear motions; but the heavenly bodies turn round a center. Thus said Aristotle.

Ptolemy of Alexandria argued that if the earth turns, making even a daily revolution, the opposite of what has been said would occur. He shows that the motion which in twenty-four hours would turn the earth would be extremely violent and of an unsurpassable velocity. But things moved with a violent rotational motion are quite unlikely to cohere, but will rather disperse in fragments—unless they are held together by a superior force. And long ago, he says, a whirling earth would have been scattered beyond the sky itself (which is wholly ridiculous), and much more so all animate beings and other separate masses, none of which could have remained stable. Furthermore, were the earth turning, freely falling bodies would never arrive perpendicularly at the points destined for them. And we would always see the clouds and other objects floating on the air moving towards the west.

VIII. *A Refutation of the Arguments Quoted, and Their Insufficiency*

For such reasons and others like them, the ancient philosophers affirmed that the earth stays always immobile at the center of the world, and that thereof there can be no doubt. But if anyone were to claim that the earth moves, he would surely say that this motion is natural and not violent. Now events occurring in conformity with nature produce results opposite to those caused by violence. Those things, indeed, to which are applied force and violence cannot long subsist and must needs soon be destroyed; but those which are in accord with nature exist in a proper way and in the best possible way.

Ptolemy therefore had no need to fear that the earth and all terrestrial beings would be destroyed by a rotation resulting from natural causes. Such a rotation wholly differs from one caused by art or by human enterprise. Why, indeed, on this head, did he not fear even more for the whole world, the motion of which would have to be as much more rapid as the heavens are greater in size than the earth? Have the heavens acquired their immensity because their motion, of an inexpressible magnitude, pulls them away from the earth? and would they fall if that motion ceased? Surely, if this reasoning were valid, the heavens would be infinite in extent. The more they are extended by the force of their motion, the more rapid would the motion become, for the distance to be traversed in twenty-four hours would be always increasing; and conversely, the immensity of the heavens would ever augment with the increase of the motion. Thus to very infinity the velocity would increase the magnitude of the motion, and the magnitude of the motion, the velocity. Then in agreement with this axiom of physics, "What is infinite cannot be traversed and cannot be moved," the heavens would necessarily halt.

It is alleged that beyond the heavens there is no body, no place, no void—nothing. Then there is only nothing into which the heavens could expand. Surely, too, it is astonishing that something should be stopped by nothing. And if the heavens are considered infinite and bounded only by an interior concavity, it is the more true that there is nothing beyond them, for everything must be within, whatever its dimensions may be. But from this argument, the heavens if infinite must be motionless; for the principal argument depended upon to show the world finite is its assumed motion.

Let us leave the philosophers to decide whether the world is finite or infinite. We are sure, in any event, that the earth between its poles is bounded by a spherical surface. Why then should we hesitate to attribute to it a motion properly according in nature with its form, rather than to disturb ourselves about the whole world, the limits of which we do not and cannot know? Shall we not therefore admit that the daily revolution belongs in reality to the earth and its appearance only to the heavens? As Virgil's Aeneas said: "We depart from the port, and the cities and lands recede."

When a ship sails along without tossing, the sailors see all things exterior to the ship moving; they see, as it were, the image of their own motion; and they think themselves and all with them to be at rest. Possibly, in the same manner, we have believed the earth to be without motion and the whole world to move round it. What then about the clouds and all other bodies floating on the air, both those which fall and those which tend to rise? Very simply, we may think that not only the earth and the aqueous element which is a part of it move thus, but also the portion—not negligible—of the air and all its contents which have a relation to the earth. Either the air neighboring the earth, mixed with aqueous and earthy materials, shares in the nature of the earth, or the motion of the air is an acquired motion in which it participates because of the contiguity of the earth and its perpetual motion. As a contrary view, it is alleged—which is astounding—that the uppermost portion of the air shares in the motions of the heavens, and thus reveals those abruptly appearing stars which the Greeks called comets or "long-haired stars" (Lat., *pogoniae*), to the formation of which this uppermost air is assigned as place, and which, like other stars, rise and set. We can reply merely that if that part of the air, because of its great distance from the earth, is freed from the aforesaid terrestrial motion, the air nearest the earth and those things suspended in it will appear to be at rest until by the wind or some other force it is buffeted hither and yon. Is not a wind in the air like a current in the water?

As to things which by their nature rise or by their nature fall, we may affirm that in relation to the world their motions may be double and are generally composed of straight lines and circles. That things earthy in their nature are drawn downward by their weight is understandable, for indubitably the parts retain the nature of the whole. For no unlike reason are fiery things drawn upwards. Consider that terrestrial fire feeds on terrestrial matter; it is even said that flame is merely glowing smoke. Now the nature of fire is to distend that of which it takes possession, and it accomplishes this expansion with such force that it cannot in any manner or by any device be prevented from performing its work once it has shattered the imprisoning bonds. But an expanding motion is directed away from the center towards the circumference. Thus if any earthy portion be kindled, it must be borne away from the center, upwards. As has been said before, for a simple body the proper motion is simple (a fact verified particularly for circular motion) as long as that body retains its individuality and rests in its natural place. In that natural place, therefore, the motion is none other than circular, the motion which is self-contained, and likest to repose. Contrarily, motion in a straight line is the act of those things which move out of their proper places, which are forced from it, or for some other reason are outside it. Now nothing is more repugnant to the form and order of the world than that something be out of its place. Therefore motion in a straight line is proper only to things which are not in order and which are not conforming to their nature—to things which are separated from their natural entities or have lost their essential individualities.

What is more, things which are impelled up or down, even neglecting their possible circular motion, do not execute a simple movement, uniform and equal. They conform consistently neither to their native lightness nor to the impulse of their weight. Those which fall execute first a slow motion which augments in velocity as they fall. Similarly, we see that terrestrial fire (and we see no other kind) as it rises simultaneously slows down, as if manifesting the force of the earthy material. Circular motion, however, always progresses in a uniform way, for it results from a constant cause. And again, things which move in straight lines soon put an end to their accelerated motion, because when they reach their destinations, they cease to be either light or heavy, and their motion stops. As, therefore, circular motion is proper to all complete, individual things, straight motion to partial things only, we may conclude that the circular motion stands toward the straight as the whole animal nature toward the sick member.

The fact that Aristotle divided simple motion into three kinds—away from the center, towards the center, and around the center—may be dismissed as merely an act of intellect. Just so, we distinguish the point, the line, and the surface, even though no one of them can exist without the others, and none of them without a body.

To all that precedes may be added that the state of immobility is usually considered more noble and more nearly divine than that of change and instability. For which is the state of rest more appropriate then, for the earth or for the world? It seems absurd to me to attribute motion to the containing and localizing rather than to the contained and localized —which is the earth.

Finally, since the planets clearly now approach and now recede from the earth, their movements being motions of single, self-contained bodies round a center, if the center of their revolutions is the center of the earth, their motion must be at one and the same time centripetal and centrifugal. Properly, one must conceive of the circular motion round a center in a more general fashion, and must be satisfied that the movement of each planet is related to its own true center.

For all the reasons given, then, motion for the earth is more probable than immobility; and especially is this true of the daily revolution, in as much as this motion is most proper for the earth. And I think that this discussion will suffice for the first part of the question.

IX. *Whether Several Motions may be Attributed to the Earth; and of the Center of the World*

SINCE then there are no reasons for our believing that the earth does not move, I think it proper now to question whether we may attribute to it several motions, whether it may not be thought of as one of the wandering stars (planets). That it is not the center of the motions of all the other heavenly bodies, their apparently unequal motions and varying distances from the earth demonstrate. For these variations cannot be explained for circular paths homocentric with the earth. But if there are several centers for these motions, it is not overbold to query whether the center of the world is the center of terrestrial gravity or some other center. For myself, I think that gravity is nothing other than a certain natural tendency given by the divine providence of the Architect of the World to the various parts so that they might assemble themselves into the one of which they are a part, coming together in the form of a globe. And it is credible that the same property belongs equally to the sun, to the moon, and to the other wandering stars. If it does, it might be thanks to its efficacy that although they travel their circuits in divers ways, they uniformly retain the roundness in which they appear.

If the earth does execute motions other than that around its center, they must be such, obviously, as will evidence themselves in many phenomena. Such a motion might be an annual progress round a circuit. If this annual motion be attributed to the earth, and if immobility be conceded to the sun, the rising and setting of the zodiacal signs and other fixed stars, thanks to which they are overhead in daytime as well as at night, will occur just as they do now. Then the progressions, halts, and retrogressions of the planets will be seen to be caused not by their motions, but by those of the earth which lends to the planets misleading appearances. Then, finally, it will have to be acknowledged that the sun occupies the center of the world.

These things both the law of the order in which they follow one after another and the harmony of the world combine to teach us, provided only that we look upon things themselves with, as it were, two eyes.

X. *Of the Order of the Heavenly Bodies*

I OBSERVE that no one questions that the heaven of the fixed stars is the highest of all which is visible. As to the order of the planets, we note that the ancient philosophers preferred to determine it according to the magnitudes of their respective revolutions. They reasoned that of bodies carried at equal speed, those which are more distant appear to be borne more slowly; this principle Euclid established in *The Optics*. They thought that as the moon completed its course in the briefest time, it was borne round the smallest circle and was therefore closest to the earth. Saturn, which in the longest time travels the greatest circuit, they considered to be the highest or most distant. Nearer than Saturn they placed Jupiter; nearer than Jupiter, Mars. About Mercury and Venus, opinions varied; for these two never, like the others, proceed far from the sun. Some thinkers, therefore, like the Timaeus of Plato, placed them beyond the sun. Others, such as Ptolemy and a number of more recent scholars, place them this side of the sun. Alpetragius places Venus beyond the sun and Mercury on this side the sun.

Now those who agree with Plato in thinking that all the stars (otherwise dark bodies) shine only by light reflected from the sun argue that because the distance of these two planets from the sun is small, if they were below the sun they would be visible to us only in part, and never entirely round. Ordinarily, they would reflect the light they receive upwards—that is, towards the sun—as we see in the new and in the waning moon. They say, too, that sometimes the sun would necessarily be hidden from us by the interposition of these planets and that its light would for us be diminished in proportion to their size as they interposed. Since such a dimming never occurs, they conclude that these planets can in no fashion ever come this side the sun.

Those who place Mercury and Venus this side the sun base their argument on the vastness of the space which they discover between the sun and the moon. They have found that the greatest distance between the earth and the moon is sixty-four and one sixtieth times the distance from the center of the earth to its surface; and that the smallest distance between the earth and the sun is almost eighteen times the greatest distance between the earth and the moon. The distance between the earth and the sun is to the distance between the moon and the sun as 1160 is to 1096. In order, therefore, that so great a space need not be considered empty and void, and judging from the distances between the planetary orbits by which they calculate the depth of these orbits, they affirm that the space would be almost filled up if the distance between Mercury and the sun were less than that between the moon and the sun, and if the distance of Venus from the sun were less than that between Mercury and the sun, each of these distances being progressively smaller. Further, in this arrangement, the highest part of the orbit of Venus would approach very close to the sun. They calculate that between the aphelion and perihelion of Mercury there would be 177 times the distance between the earth and the moon, and that the remaining distance, 910 times that between the earth and the moon, would be almost filled by the apsidal dimensions of Venus. They also do not admit that there is any opacity in the stars, asserting that these shine either by their own light or by that of the sun impregnated in their entire bodies. These planets never darken because they only very rarely interpose between us and the sun; generally, they merely skirt the sun. And because these two are small bodies—Venus is larger than Mercury, but can yet hide not a hundredth part of the sun, according to Al Bategui the Aratonian who estimates the diameter of the sun as ten times that of Venus—they believe that if either of them interposes between us and the sun, we would hardly see so small a speck in the sun's most resplendent light. Moreover, Averroes, in his paraphrase of Ptolemy, reports that he did see something blackish when he was observing the conjunction of Mercury and the sun which he had foretold by computations. Yet some persons judge that these two planets move wholly beyond the solar path.

How feeble and unsure is this reasoning becomes clear when we consider the fact that the least distance between the earth and the moon is, according to Ptolemy, thirty-eight times the distance from the earth's center to its surface (according to a better calculation, as will be shown later, more than forty-nine), yet we do not know that there is in all that space anything but air and, if it pleases us to think so, a certain fiery element. Furthermore, the diameter of the orbit of Venus, thanks to which it moves away from the sun by 45°, would have to be six times as great as the distance between the center of the earth and its perihelion, as will be demonstrated in the proper place. What do these reasoners maintain is contained in all that space, all the more that it would compass the earth, the air, the ether, the moon, and Mercury? So much must the huge epicycle of Venus embrace if that planet revolves round the motionless earth. How empty is Ptolemy's argument that the sun must occupy the mid-point between the planets moving away in all directions and those which do not depart is made clear by the moon which, itself moving away in every direction, exposes the falsity of the idea.

As to those who place Venus, then Mercury, on this side the sun, or arrange them in some other order, what reason can they allege that these do not effect the independent and different orbit of the sun, even as the other planets, unless the ratio of rapidity and slowness prevents any warping of the orbit?

It seems almost necessary to admit that the earth is not the center to which is referred the order of the stars and the orbits, even that there can be no reason for their order, and that one cannot know why the higher place belongs to Saturn rather than to Jupiter or some other planet. Perhaps that scheme is not despicable which was imagined by Martianus Capella (who wrote an encyclopedia) as well as by some other Latins. They held that Mercury and Venus revolve around the sun, which is at the center, and are unable to move further away from the sun than the convexities of their spheres permit. They thought that these two planets do not revolve round the earth, like the other planets, but have converse orbits. What can they wish to imply save that the center of these spheres is near the sun? If they are right, the sphere of Mercury is contained within that of Venus—which must be two or more times greater—and finds sufficient space within that amplitude.

Now if one should opportunely ascribe to that same center Saturn, Jupiter, and Mars—remembering that the dimensions of these spheres are such that within them they contain and embrace the earth also—he would not be far wrong; the canonic order of their motions declares it. Certainly, these planets always approach nearest to the earth when they rise at evening; that is, when they are opposite the sun, the earth being between them and the sun. Contrarily, they are most distant when they set at even; that is, when they are hidden in the sunlight, when observably the sun is between them and the earth. This phenomenon shows adequately that the center of their circuits is associated with the sun and is, in fact, the same as that round which Mercury and Venus circle in their revolutions. If the spheres of these planets have all the same center, the space which remains between the convex side of the sphere of Venus and the concave side of the sphere of Mars must form another orb or sphere homocentric with those at its two surfaces. This sphere contains the earth with its companion the moon and with all that belongs within the lunar globe. For indeed we can in no fashion separate the moon from the earth to which it is, of heavenly bodies, incontestably the nearest, and the less need we to, in that the space left for it is sufficiently vast.

Therefore we need feel no shame in affirming that all which the moon's sphere embraces, even to the center of the earth, is drawn along by the motion of the greatest sphere, first as are the spheres of the other planets, in an annual revolution round the sun. Similarly, we dare assert that the sun is the center of the world, and that the sun remains motionless, all the motion which it appears to have being truly only an image of the earth's movement. And further, we may assert that the dimensions of the world are so vast that though the distance from the sun to the earth appears very large as compared with the size of the spheres of some planets, yet compared with the dimensions of the sphere of the fixed stars, it is as nothing.

All these assertions I find it easier to admit than to shatter reason by accepting the almost infinite number of spheres which those are forced to suppose who insist that the earth is the center of the world. It surely is better to conform to the wisdom of nature. Even as she dreads producing anything superfluous or useless, she often endows one causation with several effects.

The ideas here stated are difficult, even almost impossible, to accept; they are quite contrary to popular notions. Yet with the help of God, we will make everything as clear as day in what follows, at least for those who are not ignorant of mathematics. The first law being admitted—no one can propose one more suitable—that the size of the spheres is measured by the time of their revolutions, the order of the spheres immediately results therefrom, commencing with the highest, in the following way:

The first and highest of all the spheres is the sphere of the fixed stars. It encloses all the other spheres and is itself self-contained; it is immobile; it is certainly the portion of the universe with reference to which the movement and positions of all the other heavenly bodies must be considered. If some people are yet of the opinion that this sphere moves, we are of a contrary mind; and after deducing the motion of the earth, we shall show why we so conclude. Saturn, first of the planets, which accomplishes its revolution in thirty years, is nearest to the first sphere. Jupiter, making its revolution in twelve years, is next. Then comes Mars, revolving once in two years. The fourth place in the series is occupied by the sphere which contains the earth and the sphere of the moon, and which performs an annual revolution. The fifth place is that of Venus, revolving in nine months. Finally, the sixth place is occupied by Mercury, revolving in eighty days.

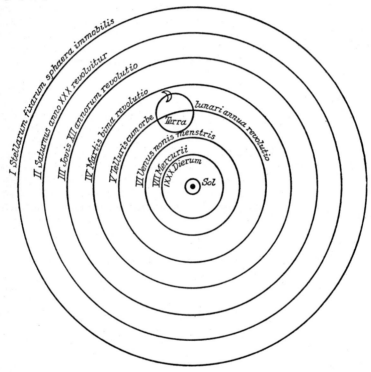

In the midst of all, the sun reposes, unmoving. Who, indeed, in this most beautiful temple would place the light-giver in any other part than that whence it can illumine all other parts? Not ineptly do some call the sun the lamp of the world, or the spirit of the world, or even the world's governor. Trismegistus calls it God visible; Sophocles' Electra, the all-seeing. Indeed, the sun, reposing as it were on a royal throne, controls the family of wandering stars which surrounds him. The earth will surely never be deprived of the ministry of the moon; as Aristotle says in *De Animalibus,* the earth and the moon enjoy the closest possible kinship. Meantime, the earth conceives by the sun and each year becomes great.

In this ordering there appears a wonderful symmetry in the world and a precise relation between the motions and sizes of the spheres which no other arrangement offers. Herein the attentive observer can see why the progress and regress of Jupiter appear greater than Saturn's and less than Mars's; why also the progress and regress of Venus appear greater than Mercury's; why Saturn appears less often in reciprocation than Jupiter, and Mercury more often than Mars and Venus; why Saturn, Jupiter, and Mars are nearer to the earth when they rise at eventide than at the time of their occultation and apparition; why Mars when it becomes pernocturnal seems to equal Jupiter in size and can be distinguished from the latter only by its reddish color, and yet at other times is scarcely discoverable among stars of the second order unless by a careful observer working with a sextant. All these phenomena arise from the same cause: the movement of the earth.

That nothing similar can be discovered among the fixed stars proves their immense distance from us, a distance so immense as to render imperceptible to us even their apparent annual motion, the image of the earth's true motion. For every visible object or event there is a distance beyond which it cannot be seen, as is proven in optics. The glitter of the fixed stars' light shows that between the highest of the planetary spheres, Saturn's, and the sphere of the fixed stars, there is still an enormous space. It is by this glitter that the fixed stars are especially distinguishable from the planets; and it is proper that between the moving and the non-moving there should be a great difference. Thus perfect, truly, are the divine works of the best and supreme Architect.

XI. *Demonstration of the Threefold Motion of the Earth*

SINCE the numerous and important evidences from the planets support the hypothesis that the earth moves, we shall now expound that motion completely and shall show how far the motion hypothesized explains the phenomena. The motion is threefold. First there is the motion which the Greeks called *nychthemeron,* as we have said, which causes the sequence of day and night. This motion is executed from west to east—as it has been believed that the world moves in a contrary sense—and is a rotation of the earth on its axis. The motion traces the equinoctial circle which some, imitating the Greek expression, name the equidiurnal.

The second motion is the annual progress of the earth's center which, with all that is attached to it, travels round the sun on the circle of the zodiac. This motion is also from west to east, and it takes place, as we have said, between the spheres of Venus and Mars. Seemingly, it is the sun which executes a similar motion. Thus, when the center of the earth passes across Capricorn, Aquarius, and so forth, the sun seems to pass Cancer, Leo, and so on.

Next it must be recognized that the equator and the axis of the earth have a variable inclination with respect to the circle of the earth's path and the plane of this circle. Were the inclination fixed, there would be no shifting inequality between days and nights; rather, at all times, there would exist the conditions of the equinox, or of the solstice, or of the shortest day, or of winter, or of summer, or of some other season. There must therefore be a third motion of the earth, varying the declination. This motion also is annual, but proceeds in a sense opposite to the motion of the center. Because these two motions are almost equal to one another but in opposite senses, the axis of the earth and the greatest of the parallel circles, the equator, face ever toward the same part of the world, as if they were motionless. Yet because of this motion of the earth, the sun appears to move obliquely on the ecliptic exactly as if the earth were the center of the world. The fact offers no difficulty provided one remembers that the distance from the earth to the sun is, compared to that from the sphere of the fixed stars, almost imperceptible.

There are matters better presented to the eye than expressed in words. I shall therefore trace the accompanying circle *a b c d* which may represent the annual motion of the earth's center in the plane of the ecliptic. In the center of the circle, *E* may represent the sun. I now cut the circle into four equal parts by means of the diameters *a E c* and *b E d* subtending equal arcs. Let us suppose that the point *a* is occupied by the beginning of Cancer, *b* by that of Libra, *c* by Capricorn, and *d* by Aries.

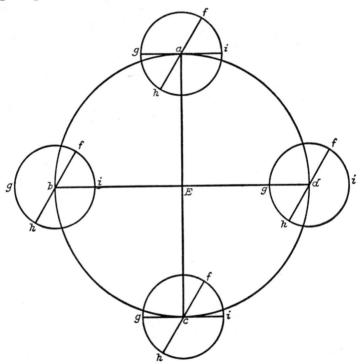

Let us also suppose that the center of the earth is, to begin with, at *a,* and let us trace the terrestrial equator *f g h i,* but not in the same plane, so that the diameter *g a i* may be common to both planes, that of the equator and that of the ecliptic. Then we shall trace similarly the diameter *f a h* at right angles to *g a i,* so that *f* shall be the limit of the greatest declination toward the south, and *h,* toward the north.

All these conditions being granted, the observer on the earth will see the sun—which is at the center *E*—in the position of the winter solstice, in Capricorn. This result arises from the greatest northern declination with respect to the sun. Conformably to the distance comprehended by the angle *E a h,* the inclination of the equator describes during the diurnal revolution the winter tropic.

Let the center of the earth now advance until it reaches the point *b,* while at the same time *f,* the limit of the greatest declination, advances in a contrary sense. Each will now have described a quarter circle. During this time, because of the equality of the two motions, the angle *E a i* will always remain equal to the angle *a E b,* and the diameters *f a h* and *g a i* will remain parallel to the diameters *f b h* and *g b i,* as will the equator. Because of the immensity of the sky, often mentioned before, they will appear the same.

Now, from the point *b*—the beginning of Libra—*E* will appear to be in Aries, and the common sections of the two circles will coincide in a single line, *g b i E.* In relation to this line, all declination is lateral, and the daily revolution reveals no declination. The sun appears to be in the position right for the spring equinox.

Let the earth continue its journey under the conditions specified until, having traveled half its route, it has reached *c.* The sun is now apparently entering Cancer. Since the southern declination of the equator, *f,* is now turned toward the sun, it will during the diurnal revolution move along the summer tropic, as measured by the angle *E c f.*

When *f* has moved through the third quadrant of the circle, the common section *g i* will coincide again with the line *E d,* and the sun will be observed in Libra; that is, the sun is at the position for the autumn equinox. Then, the same motion continuing, and *h f* turning little by little again toward the sun, there will result the original situation, that with which we started.

Another explanation. In the accompanying diagram, let *a e c* be the diameter of the ecliptic and represent the line common to the circle *a b c* and the circle of the ecliptic in the preceding diagram; this diagram is at right angles to the preceding one. In this new diagram, at *a* and at *c,* that is, in Cancer and in Capricorn, let us draw *d g f i,* which will represent a meridian of the earth, and *d f,* which will represent its axis. The north pole is at *d;* the south at *f;* and *g i* the equatorial diameter. As before, the sun is at *e.* When *f* turns toward the sun and the inclination of the equator is north by the angle *i a e,* as the earth rotates on its axis, the chord *c l* at the distance *i l* from the equator will describe the southern circle parallel to the equator. This circle appears in the sun as the tropic of Capricorn.

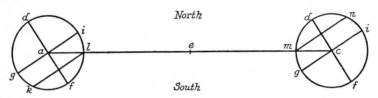

To speak more exactly, as the earth rotates on its axis, the line *a e* describes a conic section of which the apex is the center of the earth, and of which the base is parallel to the equator.

In the opposite sign of the zodiac, at *c,* precisely the same things will be true—but in the inverse sense.

It is clear, therefore, how the two mutually opposed motions—I mean those of the center and of the inclination—compel the axis of the earth to remain ever at the same inclination and in the same position. Equally clear is it that these motions appear to be motions of the sun.

We have said that the annual revolution of the center and of the inclination are almost equal. Were they precisely equal, the equinoctial and solstitial points, and the obliquity of the ecliptic with respect to the fixed stars, ought never to change. They are not precisely equal, and hence a change occurs, but so small that it is revealed only over a long period of time. For example, from Ptolemy's time to ours, the solstitial and equinoctial points have executed a precession of twenty-one degrees. From this observation, some men have argued that the sphere of the fixed stars also moves. Some talk of a ninth sphere; and as that does not suffice to explain everything, the moderns now add a tenth. They still do not attain their end. But using the movements of the earth as a principle and as a hypothesis, we hope to explain even more phenomena. If anyone maintains that the motions of the sun and of the moon can be explained on the hypothesis that the earth is immobile, the explanation offered does not accord with the motions of the other planets. Probably it was for this reason or some other similar reason—and not for the reasons alleged and refuted by Aristotle—that Philolaus admitted that it is the earth which moves. According to some authorities, Aristarchus held the same opinion.

These are matters which can, indeed, be understood only by a penetrating spirit and after long study. Knowledge of them was consequently rare among the philosophers. True, the number of those who studied the motions of the stars was very small; and it did not include Plato. And even if these matters were understood by Philolaus and some other Pythagoreans, it is not strange that their knowledge did not survive among their successors. For the Pythagoreans were not accustomed to entrust their secrets to books, or to initiate the whole world into the mysteries of philosophy. They rather confided only in their friends and kinsmen, passing their secrets on only, as it were, from hand to hand. Of this fact, the letter of Lysis to Hipparchus gives evidence. With a reference to its sentiments on secrecy, worthy to be remembered, it pleases me to end this first book.

PRINCIPIA

The Mathematical Principles of
Natural Philosophy

by

ISAAC NEWTON

CONTENTS

Principia

The Mathematical Principles of Natural Philosophy

ISAAC NEWTON

1642–1727

THE most familiar story about Isaac Newton concerns his curiosity about a falling apple and his consequent discovery of the law of gravity. This story, first recorded by Voltaire, who had it from Newton's favorite niece, may be true. It is at least not improbable; for Newton from an early age habitually observed natural phenomena closely, constantly asked "Why?" and constantly tried to set his explanations in mathematical forms.

Born on Christmas Day in 1642, the posthumous son of a freehold farmer at Woolsthorpe in Lincolnshire, Newton had his early education in small schools in his neighborhood. In 1654 he entered the grammar school at Grantham, six miles away. When he graduated from this school at the top of his class, he had, like his schoolmates, built kites and water clocks and dials; he had also contrived a four-wheeled carriage to be propelled by the occupant, and had made marked progress in mathematics. Yet when he came home to his mother—now the widow of Barnabas Smith, a clergyman—at Woolsthorpe, no one thought of any career for him but that of a small farmer. He engaged in ordinary farm routine, performed chores, went to market with his mother's agent. The agent reported that on market days the boy spent his time at bookstalls. He was frequently observed poring over mathematical treatises. Eventually his mother's brother, the rector of a parish near by, and himself a graduate of Trinity College, Cambridge, persuaded the widow Smith that her son should also go to Trinity. He was entered as a subsizar in 1661.

At Cambridge, Newton showed that he had already mastered Sanderson's *Logic,* and that, scorning Euclid as too easy to be worth studying, he had gone deep into Descartes's *Geometry.* His low opinion of Euclid he later revised; but not until after he had mastered Wallis's *Arithmetic of Infinites.*

As an undergraduate, he did make series of observations on natural phenomena such as the moon's halo, but his genius was for mathematics. In 1665 he discovered what is now known as the binomial theorem, and a little later, the elements of the differential calculus, which he called "fluxions." When, in 1668, he took his master's degree at Trinity, of which he was now a fellow, he wrote a paper which attracted the attention of the chief mathematicians of England. The following year his friend and teacher, Barrow, resigned as Lucasian professor of mathematics at Cambridge, and Newton was appointed to succeed him.

As Lucasian professor, Newton was required to lecture once a week on some portion of geometry, arithmetic, astronomy, geography, optics, statics, or other mathematical subject, and to receive students two hours a week. Choosing optics as his first topic, and later other subjects in mathematics, he lectured regularly until 1701, when he resigned his professorship. His lectures on algebra were published in 1707 by his successor in the Lucasian chair, Whiston, under the title *Arithmetica Universalis*. Other unpublished lectures may be of equal merit. Yet these years were surely productive less of great lectures than of great papers for the Royal Society.

To the Society, Newton had early sent a paper commenting on a reflecting telescope of his own invention. So well was it received that he sent other papers, several of them developed forms of ideas and discoveries really dating from his student days. In 1672, after the Royal Society had elected him to membership, there was read to it Newton's "New Theory about Light and Color," the paper in which he reported his discovery of the composition of white light. An immense controversy ensued, for Hooke, among the eminent English scientists, and Lucas and Linus, among the continental scientists, were only three of many men who violently denied the plausibility of Newton's announcement. He quietly stood his ground—content that experiment rather than argument should prove him right.

Many of Newton's papers for the Society—reports on polarization, on double refraction, on binocular vision, and so on—are now obsolete. One of them, however, developed his emission, or corpuscular, theory of light which contemporary physicists have been seriously reconsidering. And another, "De Motu," contained the germ of the *Principia*.

Celestial mechanics had been fascinating to Newton for a long time. As early as 1666, when the plague closed Cambridge and sent the undergraduate Newton home to Woolsthorpe, he was considering the possibility that gravity might extend as far as the orb of the moon. Later, to explain why the planets keep to elliptical orbits round the attracting sun, he calculated the inverse-square law. Then he applied the law to explain the path of the moon round the earth, and was dissatisfied with his computations. He convinced himself that in order to apply the law, he would first have to demonstrate mathematically that spherical bodies such as the sun and the moon act as point centers of force. By 1684, when Halley, Wren, and Hooke had all agreed on the inverse-square law—although they could not prove it—Newton had completed his calculations. He was sure now that the law applied, and he explained his solution of the great problem in "De Motu."

During the next two years Newton composed the *Principia Mathematica Philosophiae Naturalis*. In 1685 he announced his law of universal gravitation and simultaneously gave the Royal Society the first book of the *Principia*. The whole of the great work was finally published in 1687. In 1729, Andrew Motte published the first English translation; from the 1803 edition of this translation the following passages are taken.

A nervous illness—described by Pepys as "an attack of phrenitis," that is, madness—afflicted Newton in 1692. Within eighteen months he had recovered. But from the time of this illness until his death thirty-five years later, he made no great contribution to scientific knowledge. *The Opticks,* published in 1704, and Newton's only large work in English, really contains the results of studies made much earlier; and his Law of Cooling, announced to the Royal Society in 1701, he had also computed and used much earlier.

During his later years honors in abundance came to Newton. He became the president of the Royal Society in 1703, and by annual re-election held the office until his death. In 1695 he was appointed Warden of the Mint, and, in 1699, Master of the Mint. These appointments returned him many times the income he earned as Lucasian professor at Cambridge, and made possible the rather elaborate style of living he came to enjoy. Twice, in 1689 and again in 1701, he represented Cambridge as the university's member in Parliament. The French Academy made him a foreign member in 1699. In 1705, Queen Anne's consort, Prince George of Denmark, who as a member of the Royal Society greatly admired Newton and his work, persuaded the queen to knight Newton.

Unmarried, Newton seemed to enjoy equally the pleasures of London, of the Cambridge cloisters, and of his estate at Woolsthorpe. Gradually he gave more and more attention to matters not wholly scientific. He compiled a *Chronology of Ancient Kingdoms* (1728), wrote theological treatises such as *Observations on the Prophecies of Daniel,* and a *Church His-*

tory. Though his health declined as he aged, and though he suffered much from stone and gout, his mind retained such acuteness that all mathematicians deferred to him and England acknowledged him as her greatest living scientist.

The *Principia* has been for two centuries recognized as one of the world's great books. In it Newton not only sums up his own researches, but, to support them, magnificently taps the experimental and theoretical work of all the physical scholars of his and preceding times. He states definitively the first two laws of motion and adds a third, the result of his own labors; he presents and proves his Law of Universal Gravitation (see Book I, Section XII, and Book III, Proposition VIII); he shows that mass and weight are proportional to each other at any given spot on the earth (Book II, Proposition XXIV); he deduces the velocity of sound, explains the tides, traces the paths of comets, demonstrates that the sun is the center of our system, and so on.

To make the calculations upon which his generalizations rest, Newton frequently used "fluxions"—what we call calculus. But though he suggests his method in Book I, Lemmae I, II, and XI, he did not fully explain his new method until he presented it formally in 1693, in the third volume of Dr. Wallis's works. Rather, in the *Principia,* he presents everything in the Euclidean manner. From a small number of axioms he proceeds to a series of mathematical—generally geometrical—propositions and demonstrations. Thus, like Euclid and Archimedes, he moves steadily, logically, relentlessly, from the known and acknowledged to the new and surprising. As a result, until Planck announced the Quantum Theory in 1900, Newton's conclusions controlled all physical thinking; and the validity of the *Principia* remains unchallenged today within the area of gross mechanics. It is Newton's monument.

(Since terminology has changed in two centuries, the contemporary reader needs to be aware that Newton's terms must be understood as follows: *subducted,* subtracted; *conjunctly,* cross multiplied; *congress,* impact; *invention,* discovery; *used to be,* are usually; *observed the duplicate ratio,* vary as the square; *in the duplicate ratio,* as the square; *in the triplicate ratio,* as the cube; *in the sesquiplicate ratio,* as the $3/2$ power; *in the subduplicate ratio,* as the square root; *in the subtriplicate ratio,* as the cube root. Thus, in modern terminology, Book One, Section Two, Proposition IV, Corollary 2 will read: "And since the periodic times are as the radii divided by the velocities; the centripetal forces are as the radii divided by the square of the periodic times.")

PRINCIPIA

The Mathematical Principles of Natural Philosophy

DEFINITIONS

DEFINITION I

The quantity of matter is the measure of the same, arising from its density and bulk conjunctly.

THUS air of a double density, in a double space, is quadruple in quantity; in a triple space, sextuple in quantity. The same thing is to be understood of snow, and fine dust or powders, that are condensed by compression or liquefaction; and of all bodies that are by any causes whatever differently condensed. I have no regard in this place to a medium, if any such there is, that freely pervades the interstices between the parts of bodies. It is this quantity that I mean hereafter everywhere under the name of body or mass. And the same is known by the weight of each body; for it is proportional to the weight, as I have found by experiments on pendulums, very accurately made, which shall be shewn hereafter.

DEFINITION II

The quantity of motion is the measure of the same, arising from the velocity and quantity of matter conjunctly.

The motion of the whole is the sum of the motions of all the parts; and therefore in a body double in quantity, with equal velocity, the motion is double; with twice the velocity, it is quadruple.

DEFINITION III

The vis insita, *or innate force of matter, is a power of resisting, by which every body, as much as in it lies, endeavours to persevere in its pres-*

ent state, whether it be of rest, or of moving uniformly forward in a right line.

This force is ever proportional to the body whose force it is; and differs nothing from the inactivity of the mass, but in our manner of conceiving it. A body, from the inactivity of matter, is not without difficulty put out of its state of rest or motion. Upon which account, this *vis insita* may, by a most significant name, be called *vis inertiæ*, or force of inactivity. But a body exerts this force only, when another force, impressed upon it, endeavours to change its condition; and the exercise of this force may be considered both as resistance and impulse; it is resistance, in so far as the body, for maintaining its present state, withstands the force impressed; it is impulse, in so far as the body, by not easily giving way to the impressed force of another, endeavours to change the state of that other. Resistance is usually ascribed to bodies at rest, and impulse to those in motion; but motion and rest, as commonly conceived, are only relatively distinguished; nor are those bodies always truly at rest, which commonly are taken to be so.

DEFINITION IV

An impressed force is an action exerted upon a body, in order to change its state, either of rest or of moving uniformly forward in a right line.

This force consists in the action only; and remains no longer in the body, when the action is over. For a body maintains every new state it acquires, by its *vis inertiæ* only. Impressed forces are of different origins as from percussion, from pressure, from centripetal force.

DEFINITION V

A centripetal force is that by which bodies are drawn or impelled, or any way tend, towards a point as to a centre.

Of this sort is gravity, by which bodies tend to the centre of the earth; magnetism, by which iron tends to the loadstone; and that force, whatever it is, by which the planets are perpetually drawn aside from the rectilinear motions, which otherwise they would pursue, and made to revolve in curvilinear orbits. A stone, whirled about in a sling, endeavours to recede from the hand that turns it; and by that endeavour, distends the sling, and that with so much the greater force, as it is revolved with the greater velocity, and as soon as ever it is let go, flies away. That force which opposes itself to this endeavour, and by which the sling perpetually draws back the stone towards the hand, and retains it in its orbit, because it is directed to the hand as the centre of the orbit, I call the centripetal force. And the same thing is to be understood of all bodies, revolved in any orbits. They all endeavour to recede from the centres of their orbits; and were it not for the opposition of a contrary force which restrains them to, and detains them in their orbits, which I therefore call centripetal, would fly off in right lines, with an uniform motion. A projectile, if it was not for the force of gravity, would not deviate towards the earth, but would go off from it in a right line, and that with an uniform motion, if the resistance of the air was taken away. It is by its gravity that it is drawn aside perpetually from its rectilinear course, and made to deviate towards the earth, more or less, according to the force of its gravity, and the velocity of its motion. The less its gravity is, for the quantity of its matter, or the greater the velocity with which it is projected, the less will it deviate from a rectilinear course, and the farther it will go. If a leaden ball, projected from the top of a mountain by the force of gunpowder with a given velocity, and in a direction parallel to the horizon, is carried in a curve line to the distance of two miles before it falls to the ground; the same, if the resistance of the air were taken away, with a double or decuple velocity, would fly twice or ten times as far. And by increasing the velocity, we may at pleasure increase the distance to which it might be projected, and diminish the curvature of the line, which it might describe, till at last it should fall at the distance of 10, 30, or 90 degrees, or even might go quite round the whole earth before it falls; or lastly, so that it might never fall to the earth, but go forward into the celestial spaces, and proceed in its motion *in infinitum*. And after the same manner that a projectile, by the force of gravity, may be made to revolve in an orbit, and go round the whole earth, the moon also, either by the force of gravity, if it is endued with gravity, or by any other force, that impels it towards the earth, may be perpetually drawn aside towards the earth, out of the rectilinear way, which by its innate force it would pursue; and would be made to revolve in the orbit which it now describes; nor could the moon, without some such force, be retained in its orbit. If this force was too small, it would not sufficiently turn the moon out of a rectilinear course: if it was too great, it would turn it too much, and draw down the moon from its orbit towards the earth. It is necessary, that the force be of a just quantity, and it belongs to the mathematicians to find the force, that may serve exactly to retain a body in a given orbit, with a given velocity; and *vice versa*, to determine the curvilinear way, into which a body projected from a given place, with a given velocity, may be made to deviate from its natural rectilinear way, by means of a given force.

The quantity of any centripetal force may be considered as of three kinds; absolute, accelerative, and motive.

DEFINITION VI

The absolute quantity of a centripetal force is the measure of the same proportional to the efficacy of the cause that propagates it from the centre, through the spaces round about.

Thus the magnetic force is greater in one loadstone and less in another according to their sizes and strength of intensity.

DEFINITION VII

The accelerative quantity of a centripetal force is the measure of the same, proportional to the velocity which it generates in a given time.

Thus the force of the same loadstone is greater at a less distance, and less at a greater: also the force of gravity is greater in valleys, less on tops of exceeding high mountains; and yet less (as shall hereafter be shown) at greater distances from the body of the earth; but at equal distances, it is the same everywhere; because (taking away, or allowing for, the resistance of the air), it equally accelerates all falling bodies, whether heavy or light, great or small.

DEFINITION VIII

The motive quantity of a centripetal force is the measure of the same, proportional to the motion which it generates in a given time.

Thus the weight is greater in a greater body, less in a less body; and, in the same body, it is greater near to the earth, and less at remoter distances. This sort of quantity is the centripetency, or propension of the whole body towards the centre, or, as I may say, its weight; and it is always known by the quantity of an equal and contrary force just sufficient to hinder the descent of the body.

These quantities of forces, we may, for brevity's sake, call by the names of motive, accelerative, and absolute forces; and, for distinction's sake, consider them, with respect to the bodies that tend to the centre; to the places of those bodies; and to the centre of force towards which they tend; that is to say, I refer the motive force to the body as an endeavour and propensity of the whole towards a centre, arising from the propensities of the several parts taken together; the accelerative force to the place of the body, as a certain power or energy diffused from the centre to all places around to move the bodies that are in them; and the absolute force to the centre, as endued with some cause, without which those motive forces would not be propagated through the spaces round about; whether that cause be some central body (such as is the loadstone, in the centre of the magnetic force, or the earth in the centre of the gravitating force), or anything else that does not yet appear. For I here design only to give a mathematical notion of those forces, without considering their physical causes and seats.

Wherefore the accelerative force will stand in the same relation to the motive, as celerity does to motion. For the quantity of motion arises from the celerity drawn into the quantity of matter; and the motive force arises from the accelerative force drawn into the same quantity of matter. For the sum of the actions of the accelerative force, upon the several particles of the body, is the motive force of the whole. Hence it is, that near the surface of the earth, where the accelerative gravity, or force productive of gravity, in all bodies is the same, the motive gravity or the weight is as the body: but if we should ascend to higher regions, where the accelerative gravity is less, the weight would be equally diminished, and would always be as the product of the body, by the accelerative gravity. So in those regions, where the accelerative gravity is diminished into one half, the weight of a body two or three times less will be four or six times less.

I likewise call attractions and impulses, in the same sense, accelerative, and motive; and use the words attraction, impulse or propensity of any sort towards a centre, promiscuously, and indifferently, one for another; considering those forces not physically, but mathematically: wherefore, the reader is not to imagine, that by those words, I anywhere take upon me to define the kind, or the manner of any action, the causes or the physical reason thereof, or that I attribute forces, in a true and physical sense, to certain centres (which are only mathematical points); when at any time I happen to speak of centres as attracting, or as endued with attractive powers.

SCHOLIUM

Hitherto I have laid down the definitions of such words as are less known, and explained the sense in which I would have them to be understood in the following discourse. I do not define time, space, place and motion, as being well known to all. Only I must observe, that the vulgar conceive those quantities under no other notions but from the relation they bear to sensible objects. And thence arise certain prejudices, for the removing of which, it will be convenient to distinguish them into absolute and relative, true and apparent, mathematical and common.

I. Absolute, true, and mathematical time, of itself, and from its own nature, flows equably without regard to anything external, and by another name is called duration: relative, apparent, and common time is some sensible and external (whether accurate or unequable) measure of duration by the means of motion, which is commonly used instead of true time; such as an hour, a day, a month, a year.

II. Absolute space, in its own nature, without regard to anything external, remains always similar and immovable. Relative space is some movable dimension or measure of the absolute spaces; which our senses determine by its position to bodies; and which is vulgarly taken for immovable space; such is the dimension of a subterraneous, an æreal, or celestial space, determined by its position in respect of the earth. Absolute and relative space are the same in figure and magnitude; but they do not remain always numerically the same. For if the earth, for instance, moves, a space of our air, which relatively and in respect of the earth remains always the same, will at one time be one part of the absolute space into which the air passes; at another time it will be another part of the same, and so, absolutely understood, it will be perpetually mutable.

III. Place is a part of space which a body takes up, and is, according to the space, either absolute or relative. I say, a part of space; not the situation, nor the external surface of the body. For the places of equal solids are always equal; but their superficies, by reason of their dissimilar figures, are often unequal. Positions properly have no quantity, nor are they so much the places themselves, as the properties of places. The motion of the whole is the same thing with the sum of the motions of the parts; that is, the translation of the whole, out of its place, is the same thing with the sum of the translations of the parts out of their places; and therefore the place of the whole is the same thing with the sum of the places of the parts, and for that reason, it is internal, and in the whole body.

IV. Absolute motion is the translation of a body from one absolute place into another; and relative motion, the translation from one relative place into another. Thus in a ship under sail, the relative place of a body is that part of the ship which the body possesses; or that part of its cavity which the body fills, and which therefore moves together with the ship: and relative rest is the continuance of the body in the same part of the ship, or of its cavity. But real, absolute rest is the continuance of the body in the same part of that immovable space, in which the ship itself, its cavity, and all that it contains, is moved. Wherefore, if the earth is really at rest, the body, which relatively rests in the ship, will really and absolutely move with the same velocity which the ship has on the earth. But if the earth also moves, the true and absolute motion of the body will arise, partly from the true motion of the earth, in immovable space; partly from the relative motion of the ship on the earth; and if the body moves also relatively in the ship its true motion will arise, partly from the true motion of the earth, in immovable space, and partly from the relative motions as well of the ship on the earth, as of the body in the ship; and from these relative motions will arise the relative motion of the body on the earth. As if that part of the earth, where the ship is, was truly moved toward the east, with a velocity of 10010 parts; while the ship itself, with a fresh gale, and full sails, is carried towards the west, with a velocity expressed by 10 of those parts; but a sailor walks in the ship towards the east, with 1 part of the said velocity; then the sailor will be moved truly in immovable space towards the east, with a velocity of 10001 parts, and relatively on the earth towards the west, with a velocity of 9 of those parts.

Absolute time, in astronomy, is distinguished from relative, by the equation or correction of the vulgar time. For the natural days are truly unequal, though they are commonly considered as equal, and used for a measure of time; astronomers correct this inequality for their more accurate deducing of the celestial motions. It may be that there is no such thing as an equable motion, whereby time may be accurately measured. All motions may be accelerated and retarded, but the true, or equable, progress of absolute time is liable to no change. The duration or perseverance of the existence of things remains the same, whether the motions are swift or slow, or none at all: and therefore it ought to be distinguished from what are only sensible measures thereof; and out of which we collect it, by means of the astronomical equation. The necessity of which equation, for determining the times of a phænomenon, is evinced as well from the experiments of the pendulum clock, as by eclipses of the satellites of *Jupiter.*

As the order of the parts of time is immutable, so also is the order of the parts of space. Suppose those parts to be moved out of their places, and they will be moved (if the expression may be allowed) out of themselves. For times and spaces are, as it were, the places as well of themselves as of all other things. All things are placed in time as to order of succession; and in space as to order of situation. It is from their essence or nature that they are places; and that the primary places of things should be movable is absurd. These are therefore the absolute places; and translations out of those places are the only absolute motions.

But because the parts of space cannot be seen, or distinguished from one another by our senses, therefore in their stead we use sensible measures of them. For from the positions and distances of things from any body considered as immovable, we define all places; and then with respect to such places, we estimate all motions, considering bodies as transferred from some of those places into others. And so, instead of absolute places and motions, we use relative ones; and that without any inconvenience in common affairs; but in philosophical disquisitions, we ought to abstract from our senses, and consider things themselves, distinct from what are only sensible measures of them. For it may be that there is no body really at rest, to which the places and motions of others may be referred.

But we may distinguish rest and motion, absolute and relative, one from the other by their properties, causes and effects. It is a property of rest, that bodies really at rest do rest in respect to one another. And therefore as it is possible, that in the remote regions of the fixed stars, or perhaps far beyond them, there may be some body absolutely at rest; but impossible to know, from the position of bodies to one another in our regions, whether any of these do keep the same position to that remote body; it follows that absolute rest cannot be determined from the position of bodies in our regions.

It is a property of motion, that the parts, which retain given positions to their wholes, do partake of the motions of those wholes. For all the parts of revolving bodies endeavour to recede from the axis of motion; and the impetus of bodies moving forward arises from the joint impetus of all the parts. Therefore, if surrounding bodies are moved, those that are relatively at rest within them will partake of their motion. Upon which account, the true and absolute motion of a body cannot be determined by the translation of it from those which only seem to rest; for the external bodies ought not only to appear at rest, but to be really at rest. For otherwise, all included bodies, beside their translation from near the surrounding ones, partake likewise of their true motions; and though that translation were not made they would not be really at rest, but only seem to be so. For the surrounding bodies stand in the like relation to the surrounded as the exterior part of a whole does to the interior, or as the shell does to the kernel; but, if the shell moves, the kernel will also move, as being part of the whole, without any removal from near the shell.

A property, near akin to the preceding, is this, that if a place is moved, whatever is placed therein moves along with it; and therefore a body, which is moved from a place in motion, partakes also of the motion of its place. Upon which account, all motions, from places in motion, are no other than parts of entire and absolute motions; and every entire motion is composed of the motion of the body out of its first place, and the motion of this place out of its place; and so on, until we come to some immovable place, as in the before-mentioned example of the sailor. Wherefore, entire and absolute motions can be no otherwise determined than by immovable places; and for that reason I did before refer those absolute motions to immovable places, but relative ones to movable places. Now no other places are immovable but those that, from infinity to infinity, do all retain the same given position one to another; and upon this account must ever remain unmoved; and do thereby constitute immovable space.

The causes by which true and relative motions are distinguished, one from the other, are the forces impressed upon bodies to generate motion. True motion is neither generated nor altered, but by some force impressed upon the body moved; but relative motion may be generated or altered without any force impressed upon the body. For it is sufficient only to impress some force on other bodies with which the former is compared, that by their giving way, that relation may be changed, in which the relative rest or motion of this other body did consist. Again, true motion suffers always some change from any force impressed upon the moving body; but relative motion does not necessarily undergo any change by such forces. For if the same forces are likewise impressed on those other bodies, with which the comparison is made, that the relative position may be preserved, then that condition will be preserved in which the relative motion consists. And therefore any relative motion may be changed when the true motion remains unaltered, and the relative may be preserved when the true suffers some change. Upon which accounts, true motion does by no means consist in such relations.

The effects which distinguish absolute from relative motion are the forces of receding from the axis of circular motion. For there are no such forces in a circular motion purely relative, but in a true and absolute circular motion they are greater or less, according to the quantity of the motion. If a vessel, hung by a long cord, is so often turned about that the cord is strongly twisted, then filled with water, and held at rest together with the water; after, by the sudden action of another force, it is whirled about the contrary way, and while the cord is untwisting itself, the vessel continues for some time in this motion; the surface of the water will at first be plain, as before the vessel began to move; but the vessel, by gradually communicating its motion to the water, will make it begin sensibly to revolve, and recede by little and little from the middle, and ascend to the sides of the vessel, forming itself into a concave figure (as I have ex-perienced), and the swifter the motion becomes, the higher will the water rise, till at last, performing its revolutions in the same times with the vessel, it becomes relatively at rest in it. This ascent of the water shows its endeavour to recede from the axis of its motion; and the true and absolute circular motion of the water, which is here directly contrary to the relative, discovers itself, and may be measured by this endeavour. At first, when the relative motion of the water in the vessel was greatest, it produced no endeavour to recede from the axis; the water showed no tendency to the circumference, nor any ascent towards the sides of the vessel, but remained of a plain surface, and therefore its true circular motion had not yet begun. But afterwards, when the relative motion of the water had decreased, the ascent thereof towards the sides of the vessel proved its endeavour to recede from the axis; and this endeavour showed the real circular motion of the water perpetually increasing, till it had acquired its greatest quantity, when the water rested relatively in the vessel. And therefore this endeavour does not depend upon any translation of the water in respect of the ambient bodies, nor can true circular motion be defined by such translation. There is only one real circular motion of any one revolving body, corresponding to only one power of endeavouring to recede from its axis of motion, as its proper and adequate effect; but relative motions, in one and the same body, are innumerable, according to the various relations it bears to external bodies, and, like other relations, are altogether destitute of any real effect, any otherwise than they may perhaps partake of that one only true motion. And therefore in their system who suppose that our heavens, revolving below the sphere of the fixed stars, carry the planets along with them; the several parts of those heavens, and the planets, which are indeed relatively at rest in their heavens, do yet really move. For they change their position one to another (which never happens to bodies truly at rest), and being carried together with their heavens, partake of their motions, and as parts of revolving wholes, endeavour to recede from the axis of their motions.

Wherefore relative quantities are not the quantities themselves, whose names they bear, but those sensible measures of them (either accurate or inaccurate), which are commonly used instead of the measured quantities themselves. And if the meaning of words is to be determined by their use, then by the names time, space, place and motion, their measures are properly to be understood; and the expression will be unusual, and purely mathematical, if the measured quantities themselves are meant. Upon which account, they do strain the sacred writings, who there interpret those words for the measured quantities. Nor do those less defile the purity of mathematical and philosophical truths, who confound real quantities themselves with their relations and vulgar measures.

It is indeed a matter of great difficulty to discover, and effectually to distinguish, the true motions of particular bodies from the apparent; because the parts of that immovable space, in which those motions are performed, do by no means come under the observation of our senses. Yet the thing is not altogether desperate; for we have some arguments to guide us, partly from the apparent motions, which are the differences of the true motions; partly from the forces, which are the causes and effects of the true motions. For instance, if two globes, kept at a given distance one from the other by means of a cord that connects them, were revolved about their common centre of gravity, we might, from the tension of the cord, discover the endeavour of the globes to recede from the axis of their motion, and from thence we might compute the quantity of their circular motions. And then if any equal forces should be impressed at once on the alternate faces of the globes to augment or diminish their circular motions, from the increase or decrease of the tension of the cord, we might infer the increment or decrement of their motions; and thence would be found on what faces those forces ought to be impressed, that the motions of the globes might be most augmented; that is, we might discover their hindermost faces, or those which, in the circular motion, do follow. But the faces which follow being known, and consequently the opposite ones that precede, we should likewise know the determination of their motions. And thus we might find both the quantity and the determination of this circular motion, even in an immense vacuum, where there was nothing external or sensible with which the globes could be compared. But now, if in that space some remote bodies were placed that kept always a given position one to another, as the fixed stars do in our regions, we could not indeed determine, from the relative translation of the globes among those bodies, whether the motion did belong to the globes or to the bodies. But if we observed the cord, and found that its tension was that very tension which the motions of the globes required, we might conclude the motion to be in the globes, and the bodies to be at rest; and then, lastly, from the translation of the globes among the bodies, we should find the determination of their motions. But how we are to collect the true motions from their causes, effects, and apparent differences; and, *vice versa,* how from the motions, either true or apparent, we may come to the knowledge of their causes and effects, shall be explained more at large in the following tract. For to this end it was that I composed it.

AXIOMS, OR LAWS OF MOTION

LAW I

Every body perseveres in its state of rest, or of uniform motion in a right line, unless it is compelled to change that state by forces impressed thereon.

Projectiles persevere in their motions, so far as they are not retarded by the resistance of the air, or impelled downwards by the force of gravity. A top, whose parts by their cohesion are perpetually drawn aside from rectilinear motions, does not cease its rotation, otherwise than as it is retarded by the air. The greater bodies of the planets and comets, meeting with less resistance in more free spaces, preserve their motions both progressive and circular for a much longer time.

LAW II

The alteration of motion is ever proportional to the motive force impressed; and is made in the direction of the right line in which that force is impressed.

If any force generates a motion, a double force will generate double the motion, a triple force triple the motion, whether that force be impressed altogether and at once, or gradually and successively. And this motion (being always directed the same way with the generating force), if the body moved before, is added to or subducted from the former motion, according as they directly conspire with or are directly contrary to each other; or obliquely joined, when they are oblique, so as to produce a new motion compounded from the determination of both.

LAW III

To every action there is always opposed an equal reaction: or the mutual actions of two bodies upon each other are always equal, and directed to contrary parts.

Whatever draws or presses another is as much drawn or pressed by that other. If you press a stone with your finger, the finger is also pressed by the stone. If a horse draws a stone tied to a rope, the horse (if I may so say) will be equally drawn back towards the stone: for the distended rope, by the same endeavour to relax or unbend itself, will draw the horse as much towards the stone, as it does the stone towards the horse, and will obstruct the progress of the one as much as it advances that of the other. If a body impinge upon another, and by its force change the motion of the other, that body also (because of the equality of the mutual pressure) will undergo an equal change, in its own motion, towards the contrary part. The changes made by these actions are equal, not in the velocities but in the motions of bodies; that is to say, if the bodies are not hindered by any other impediments. For, because the motions are equally changed, the changes of the velocities made towards contrary parts are reciprocally proportional to the bodies. This law takes place also in attractions.

COROLLARY I

A body by two forces conjoined will describe the diagonal of a parallelogram, in the same time that it would describe the sides, by those forces apart.

If a body in a given time, by the force M impressed apart in the place A, should with an uniform motion be carried from A to B; and by the force N impressed apart in the same place, should be carried from A to C; complete the parallelogram ABCD, and, by both forces acting together, it will in the same time be carried in the diagonal from A to D. For since the force N acts in the direction of the line AC, parallel to BD, this force (by the second law) will not at all alter the velocity generated by the other force M, by which the body is carried towards the line BD. The body therefore will arrive at the line BD in the same time, whether the force N be impressed or not; and therefore at the end of that time it

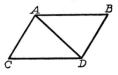

will be found somewhere in the line BD. By the same argument, at the end of the same time it will be found somewhere in the line CD. Therefore it will be found in the point D, where both lines meet. But it will move in a right line from A to D, by Law I.

COROLLARY II

And hence is explained the composition of any one direct force AD, out of any two oblique forces AC and CD; and, on the contrary, the resolution of any one direct force AD into two oblique forces AC and CD: which composition and resolution are abundantly confirmed from mechanics.

COROLLARY III

The quantity of motion, which is collected by taking the sum of the motions directed towards the same parts, and the difference of those that are directed to contrary parts, suffers no change from the action of bodies among themselves.

For action and its opposite re-action are equal, by Law III, and therefore, by Law II, they produce in the motions equal changes towards opposite parts. Therefore if the motions are directed towards the same parts, whatever is added to the motion of the preceding body will be subducted from the motion of that which follows; so that the sum will be the same as before. If the bodies meet, with contrary motions, there will be an equal deduction from the motions of both; and therefore the difference of the motions directed towards opposite parts will remain the same. Thus if a spherical body A with two parts of velocity is triple of a spherical body B which follows in the same right line with ten parts of velocity, the motion of A will be to that of B as 6 to 10. Suppose, then, their motions to be of 6 parts and of 10 parts, and the sum will be 16 parts. Therefore, upon the meeting of the bodies, if A acquire 3, 4, or 5 parts of motion, B will lose as many; and therefore after reflexion A will proceed with 9, 10, or 11 parts, and B with 7, 6, or 5 parts; the sum remaining always of 16 parts as before. If the body A acquire 9, 10, 11, or 12 parts of motion, and therefore after meeting proceed with 15, 16, 17, or 18 parts, the body B, losing so many parts as A has got, will either proceed with 1 part, having lost 9, or stop and remain at rest, as having lost its whole progressive motion of 10 parts; or it will go back with 1 part, having not only lost its whole motion, but (if I may so say) one part more; or it will go back with 2 parts, because a progressive motion of 12 parts is taken off. And so the sums of the conspiring motions 15+1, or 16+0, and the differences of the contrary motions 17—1 and 18—2, will always be equal to 16 parts, as they were before the meeting and reflexion of the bodies. But, the motions being known with which the bodies proceed after reflexion, the velocity of either will be also known, by taking the velocity after to the velocity before reflexion, as the motion after is to the motion before. As in the last case, where the motion of the body A was of 6 parts before reflexion and of 18 parts after, and the velocity was of 2 parts before reflexion, the velocity thereof after reflexion will be found to be of 6 parts; by saying, as the 6 parts of motion before to 18 parts after, so are 2 parts of velocity before reflexion to 6 parts after.

But if the bodies are either not spherical, or, moving in different right lines, impinge obliquely one upon the other, and their motions after reflexion are required, in those cases we are first to determine the position of the plane that touches the concurring bodies in the point of concourse, then the motion of each body (by Corol. II) is to be resolved into two, one perpendicular to that plane, and the other parallel to it. This done, because the bodies act upon each other in the direction of a line perpendicular to this plane, the parallel motions are to be retained the same after reflexion as before; and to the perpendicular motions we are to assign equal changes towards the contrary parts; in such manner that the sum of the conspiring and the difference of the contrary motions may remain the same as before. From such kind of reflexions also sometimes arise the circular motions of bodies about their own centres. But these are cases which I do not consider in what follows; and it would be too tedious to demonstrate every particular that relates to this subject.

COROLLARY IV

The common centre of gravity of two or more bodies does not alter its state of motion or rest by the actions of the bodies among themselves; and therefore the common centre of gravity of all bodies acting upon each other (excluding outward actions and impediments) is either at rest or moves uniformly in a right line.

COROLLARY V

The motions of bodies included in a given space are the same among themselves, whether that space is at rest or moves uniformly forwards in a right line without any circular motion.

For the differences of the motions tending towards the same parts, and the sums of those that tend towards contrary parts, are, at first (by supposition), in both cases the same; and it is from those sums and differences that the collisions and impulses do arise with which the bodies mutually impinge one upon another. Wherefore (by Law II), the effects of those collisions will be equal in both cases; and therefore the mutual motions of the bodies among themselves in the one case will remain equal to the mutual motions of the bodies among themselves in the other. A clear proof of which we have from the experiment of a ship; where all motions happen after the same manner, whether the ship is at rest or is carried uniformly forwards in a right line.

COROLLARY VI

If bodies, any how moved among themselves, are urged in the direction of parallel lines by equal accelerative forces, they will all continue to move among themselves, after the same manner as if they had been urged by no such forces.

For these forces acting equally (with respect to the quantities of the bodies to be moved), and in the direction of parallel lines, will (by Law II) move all the bodies equally (as to velocity), and therefore will never produce any change in the positions or motions of the bodies among themselves.

SCHOLIUM

Hitherto I have laid down such principles as have been received by mathematicians, and are confirmed by abundance of experiments. By the first two Laws and the first two Corollaries, Galileo discovered that the descent of bodies observed the duplicate ratio of the time, and that the motion of projectiles was in the curve of a parabola; experience agreeing with both, unless so far as these motions are a little retarded by the resistance of the air. When a body is falling, the uniform force of its gravity, acting equally, impresses, in equal particles of time, equal forces upon that body, and therefore generates equal velocities; and in the whole time impresses a whole force, and generates a whole velocity proportional to the time. And the spaces described in proportional times are as the velocities and the times conjunctly; that is, in a duplicate ratio of the times. And when a body is thrown upwards, its uniform gravity impresses forces and takes off velocities proportional to the times; and the times of ascending to the greatest heights are as the velocities to be taken off, and those heights are as the velocities and the times conjunctly, or in the duplicate ratio of the velocities. And if a body be projected in any direction, the motion arising from its projection is compounded with the motion arising from its gravity. As if the body A by its motion of projection alone could describe in a given time the right line AB, and with its motion of falling alone could describe in the same time the altitude AC; complete the parallelogram ABDC, and the body by that compounded motion will at the end of the time be found in the place D; and the curve line AED, which that body describes, will be a parabola, to

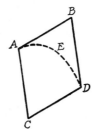

which the right line AB will be a tangent in A; and whose ordinate BD will be as the square of the line AB. On the same Laws and Corollaries depend those things which have been demonstrated concerning the times of the vibration of pendulums, and are confirmed by the daily experiments of pendulum clocks. By the same, together with the third Law, Sir Christ. Wren, Dr. Wallis, and Mr. Huygens, the greatest geometers of our times, did severally determine the rules of the congress and reflexion of hard bodies, and much about the same time communicated their discoveries to the Royal Society, exactly agreeing among themselves as to those rules. Dr. Wallis, indeed, was something more early in the publication; then followed Sir Christopher Wren, and, lastly, Mr. Huygens. But Sir Christopher Wren confirmed the truth of the thing before the Royal Society by the experiment of pendulums, which Mr. Mariotte soon after thought fit to explain in a treatise entirely upon that subject.

Book One: Of the Motion of Bodies

SECTION ONE

Of the method of first and last ratios of quantities, by the help whereof we demonstrate the propositions that follow.

LEMMA I

Quantities, and the ratios of quantities, which in any finite time converge continually to equality, and before the end of that time approach nearer the one to the other than by any given difference, become ultimately equal.

If you deny it, suppose them to be ultimately unequal, and let D be their ultimate difference. Therefore they cannot approach nearer to equality than by that given difference D; which is against the supposition.

LEMMA II

If in any figure AacE, *terminated by the right lines* Aa, AE, *and the curve* acE, *there be inscribed any number of parallelograms* Ab, Bc, Cd, &c., *comprehended under equal bases* AB, BC, CD, &c., *and the sides,*

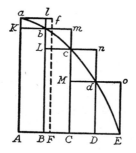

Bb, Cc, Dd, &c., *parallel to one side* Aa *of the figure; and the parallelograms* aKbl, bLcm, cMdn, &c., *are completed. Then if the breadth of those parallelograms be supposed to be diminished, and their number to be augmented* in infinitum; *I say, that the ultimate ratios which the inscribed figure* AKbLcMdD, *the circumscribed figure* Aalbmcn-doE, *and curvilinear figure* AabcdE *will have to one another are ratios of equality.*

For the difference of the inscribed and circumscribed figures is the sum of the parallelograms K*l*, L*m*, M*n*, D*o*, that is (from the equality of all their bases), the rectangle under one of their bases K*b* and the sum of their altitudes A*a*, that is, the rectangle AB*la*. But this rectangle, because its breadth AB is supposed diminished *in infinitum*, becomes less than any given space. And therefore (by Lem. I) the figures inscribed and circumscribed become ultimately equal one to the other; and much more will the intermediate curvilinear figure be ultimately equal to either. Q.E.D.

LEMMA III

The same ultimate ratios are also ratios of equality, when the breadths, AB, BC, DC, &c., of the parallelograms are unequal, and are all diminished in infinitum.

For suppose AF equal to the greatest breadth, and complete the parallelogram FA*af*. This parallelogram will be greater than the difference of the inscribed and circumscribed figures; but, because its breadth AF is

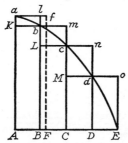

diminished *in infinitum*, it will become less than any given rectangle. Q.E.D.

Cor. 1. Hence the ultimate sum of those evanescent parallelograms will in all parts coincide with the curvilinear figure.

Cor. 2. Much more will the rectilinear figure comprehended under the chords of the evanescent arcs *ab, bc, cd*, &c., ultimately coincide with the curvilinear figure.

Cor. 3. And also the circumscribed rectilinear figure comprehended under the tangents of the same arcs.

Cor. 4. And therefore these ultimate figures (as to their perimeters *ac*E) are not rectilinear, but curvilinear limits of rectilinear figures.

LEMMA IV

If in two figures AacE, PprT, you inscribe (as before) two ranks of parallelograms, an equal number in each rank, and, when their breadths are diminished in infinitum, the ultimate ratios of the parallelograms in one figure to those in the other, each to each respectively, are the same; I say, that those two figures AacE, PprT, are to one another in that same ratio.

For as the parallelograms in the one are severally to the parallelograms in the other, so (by composition) is the sum of all in the one to the sum of all in the other; and so is the one figure to the other; because (by Lem. III) the former figure to the former sum, and the latter figure to the latter sum, are both in the ratio of equality. Q.E.D.

Cor. Hence if two quantities of any kind are any how divided into an equal number of parts, and those parts, when their number is augmented, and their magnitude diminished *in infinitum,* have a given ratio one to the other, the first to the first, the second to the second, and so on

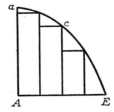 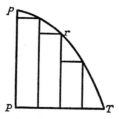

in order, the whole quantities will be one to the other in that same given ratio. For if, in the figures of this Lemma, the parallelograms are taken one to the other in the ratio of the parts, the sum of the parts will always be as the sum of the parallelograms; and therefore supposing the number of the parallelograms and parts to be augmented, and their magnitudes diminished *in infinitum,* those sums will be in the ultimate ratio of the parallelogram in the one figure to the correspondent parallelogram in the other; that is (by the supposition), in the ultimate ratio of any part of the one quantity to the correspondent part of the other.

LEMMA V

In similar figures, all sorts of homologous sides, whether curvilinear or rectilinear, are proportional· and the areas are in the duplicate ratio of the homologous sides.

LEMMA VI

If any arc ACB, given in position, is subtended by its chord AB, and in any point A, in the middle of the continued curvature, is touched by a right line AD, produced both ways; then if the points A and B approach one another and meet, I say, the angle BAD, contained between the chord and the tangent, will be diminished in infinitum, *and ultimately will vanish.*

For if that angle does not vanish, the arc ACB will contain with the tangent AD an angle equal to a rectilinear angle; and therefore the curvature at the point A will not be continued, which is against the supposition.

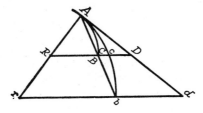

LEMMA VII

The same things being supposed, I say that the ultimate ratio of the arc, chord, and tangent, any one to any other, is the ratio of equality.

For while the point B approaches towards the point A, consider always AB and AD as produced to the remote points *b* and *d*, and parallel to the secant BD draw *bd*: and let the arc A*cb* be always similar to the arc ACB. Then, supposing the points A and B to coincide, the angle *dAb* will vanish, by the preceding Lemma; and therefore the right lines A*b*, A*d* (which are always finite), and the intermediate arc A*cb*, will coincide, and become equal among themselves. Wherefore, the right lines AB, AD, and the intermediate arc ACB (which are always proportional to the former), will vanish, and ultimately acquire the ratio of equality. Q.E.D.

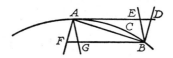

Cor. 1. Whence if through B we draw BF parallel to the tangent, always cutting any right line AF passing through A in F, this line BF will ultimately be in the ratio of equality with the evanescent arc ACB; because, completing the parallelogram AFBD, it is always in a ratio of equality with AD.

Cor. 2. And if through B and A more right lines are drawn, as BE, BD, AF, AG, cutting the tangent AD and its parallel BF; the ultimate ratio of all the abscissas AD, AE, BF, BG, and of the chord and arc AB, any one to any other, will be the ratio of equality.

Cor. 3. And therefore in all our reasoning about ultimate ratios, we may freely use any one of those lines for any other.

LEMMA VIII

If the right lines AR, BR, *with the arc* ACB, *the chord* AB, *and the tangent* AD, *constitute three triangles* RAB, RACB, RAD, *and the points* A *and* B *approach and meet: I say, that the ultimate form of these evanescent triangles is that of similitude, and their ultimate ratio that of equality.*

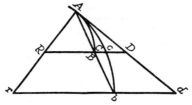

Cor. And hence in all reasonings about ultimate ratios, we may indifferently use any one of those triangles for any other.

LEMMA IX

If a right line AE, *and a curve line* ABC, *both given by position, cut each other in a given angle,* A; *and to that right line, in another given angle,* BD, CE *are ordinately applied, meeting the curve in* B, C; *and the points* B *and* C *together approach towards and meet in the point* A: *I say, that the areas of the triangles* ABD, ACE, *will ultimately be one to the other in the duplicate ratio of the sides.*

LEMMA X

The spaces which a body describes by any finite force urging it, whether that force is determined and immutable, or is continually augmented or continually diminished, are in the very beginning of the motion one to the other in the duplicate ratio of the times.

Cor. 1. And hence one may easily infer, that the errors of bodies describing similar parts of similar figures in proportional times are nearly as the squares of the times in which they are generated; if so be these errors are generated by any equal forces similarly applied to the bodies, and measured by the distances of the bodies from those places of the similar figures, at which, without the action of those forces, the bodies would have arrived in those proportional times.

Cor. 2. But the errors that are generated by proportional forces, similarly applied to the bodies at similar parts of the similar figures, are as the forces and the squares of the times conjunctly.

Cor. 3. The same thing is to be understood of any spaces whatsoever described by bodies urged with different forces; all which, in the very beginning of the motion, are as the forces and the squares of the times conjunctly.

Cor. 4. And therefore the forces are as the spaces described in the very beginning of the motion directly, and the squares of the times inversely.

Cor. 5. And the squares of the times are as the spaces described directly, and the forces inversely.

LEMMA XI

The evanescent subtense of the angle of contact, in all curves which at the point of contact have a finite curvature, is ultimately in the duplicate ratio of the subtense of the conterminate arc.

CASE 1. Let AB be that arc, AD its tangent, BD the subtense of the angle of contact perpendicular on the tangent, AB the subtense of the arc. Draw BG perpendicular to the subtense AB, and AG to the tangent AD, meeting in G; then let the points D, B, and G approach to the points *d, b,* and *g,* and suppose J to be the ultimate intersection of the lines BG, AG, when the points D, B, have come to A. It is evident that the distance GJ may be less than any assignable. But (from the nature of the circles passing through the points A, B, G, A, *b, g,*) $AB^2 = AG \times BD$, and $Ab^2 = Ag \times bd;$ and therefore the ratio of AB^2 to Ab^2 is compounded of the ratios of AG to A*g,* and of B*d* to *bd*. But because GJ may be assumed of less length than any assignable, the ratio of AG to A*g* may be such as to differ from the ratio of equality by less than any assignable difference; and therefore the ratio 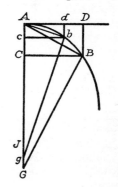 of AB^2 to Ab^2 may be such as to differ from the ratio of BD to *bd* by less than any assignable difference. Therefore, by Lem. I, the ultimate ratio of AB^2 to Ab^2 is the same with the ultimate ratio of BD to *bd*. Q.E.D.

CASE 2. Now let BD be inclined to AD in any given angle, and the ultimate ratio of BD to *bd* will always be the same as before, and therefore the same with the ratio of AB^2 to Ab^2. Q.E.D.

CASE 3. And if we suppose the angle D not to be given, but that the right line BD converges to a given point, or is determined by any other condition whatever; nevertheless the angles D, *d,* being determined by the same law, will always draw nearer to equality, and approach nearer to each other than by any assigned difference, and therefore, by Lem. I, will at last be equal; and therefore the lines BD, *bd* are in the same ratio to each other as before. Q.E.D.

Cor. 1. Therefore since the tangents AD, A*d,* the arcs AB, A*b,* and their sines, BC, *bc,* become ultimately equal to the chords AB, A*b,* their squares will ultimately become as the subtenses BD, *bd.*

Cor. 2. Their squares are also ultimately as the versed sines of the arcs, bisecting the chords, and converging to a given point. For those versed sines are as the subtenses BD, *bd.*

Cor. 3. And therefore the versed sine is in the duplicate ratio of the time in which a body will describe the arc with a given velocity.

Cor. 4. The rectilinear triangles ADB, A*db* are ultimately in the triplicate ratio of the sides AD, A*d,* and in a sesquiplicate ratio of the sides DB, *db;* as being in the ratio compounded of the sides AD to DB, and of A*d* to *db.* So also the triangles ABC, A*bc* are ultimately in the triplicate ratio of the sides BC, *bc.* What I call the sesquiplicate ratio is the subduplicate of the triplicate, as being compounded of the simple and subduplicate ratio.

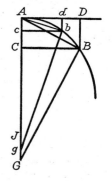

Cor. 5. And because DB, *db* are ultimately parallel and in the duplicate ratio of the lines AD, A*d,* the ultimate curvilinear areas ADB, A*db* will be (by the nature of the parabola) two thirds of the rectilinear triangles ADB, A*db* and the segments AB, A*b* will be one third of the same triangles. And thence those areas and those segments will be in the triplicate ratio as well of the tangents AD, A*d,* as of the chords and arcs AB, A*b.*

SCHOLIUM

But we have all along supposed the angle of contact to be neither infinitely greater nor infinitely less than the angles of contact made by circles and their tangents; that is, that the curvature at the point A is neither infinitely small nor infinitely great, or that the interval AJ is of a finite magnitude. For DB may be taken as AD^3: in which case no circle can be drawn through the point A, between the tangent AD and the curve AB, and therefore the angle of contact will be infinitely less than those of circles. And by a like reasoning, if DB be made successively as AD^4, AD^5, AD^6, AD^7, &c., we shall have a series of angles of contact, proceeding *in infinitum,* wherein every succeeding term is infinitely less than the preceding. And if DB be made successively as AD^2, $AD^{4/3}$, $AD^{4/5}$, $AD^{5/4}$, $AD^{6/5}$, $AD^{7/6}$, &c., we shall have another infinite series of angles of contact, the first of which is of the same sort with those of circles, the second infinitely greater, and every succeeding one infinitely greater than the preceding. But between any two of these angles another series of intermediate angles of contact may be interposed, proceeding both ways *in infinitum,* wherein every succeeding angle shall be infinitely greater or infinitely less than the preceding. As if between the terms AD^2 and AD^3 there were interposed the series $AD^{13/6}$, $AD^{11/5}$, $AD^{9/4}$, $AD^{7/3}$, $AD^{5/2}$,

$AD^{8}\!/_{3}$, $AD^{1}\!1\!/_{4}$, $AD^{1}\!4\!/_{5}$, $AD^{1}\!7\!/_{6}$, &c. And again, between any two angles of this series, a new series of intermediate angles may be interposed, differing from one another by infinite intervals. Nor is nature confined to any bounds.

Those things which have been demonstrated of curve lines, and the superficies which they comprehend, may be easily applied to the curve superficies and contents of solids. These Lemmas are premised to avoid the tediousness of deducing perplexed demonstrations *ad absurdum,* according to the method of the ancient geometers. For demonstrations are more contracted by the method of indivisibles: but because the hypothesis of indivisibles seems somewhat harsh, and therefore that method is reckoned less geometrical, I chose rather to reduce the demonstrations of the following propositions to the first and last sums and ratios of nascent and evanescent quantities, that is, to the limits of those sums and ratios; and so to premise, as short as I could, the demonstrations of those limits. For hereby the same thing is performed as by the method of indivisibles; and now those principles being demonstrated, we may use them with more safety. Therefore if hereafter I should happen to consider quantities as made up of particles, or should use little curve lines for right ones, I would not be understood to mean indivisibles, but evanescent divisible quantities; not the sums and ratios of determinate parts, but always the limits of sums and ratios; and that the force of such demonstrations always depends on the method laid down in the foregoing Lemmas.

Perhaps it may be objected that there is no ultimate proportion of evanescent quantities; because the proportion, before the quantities have vanished, is not the ultimate, and when they are vanished, is none. But by the same argument, it may be alleged that a body arriving at a certain place, and there stopping, has no ultimate velocity: because the velocity, before the body comes to the place, is not its ultimate velocity; when it has arrived, is none. But the answer is easy; for by the ultimate velocity is meant that with which the body is moved, neither before it arrives at its last place and the motion ceases, nor after, but at the very instant it arrives; that is, that velocity with which the body arrives at its last place, and with which the motion ceases. And in like manner, by the ultimate ratio of evanescent quantities is to be understood the ratio of the quantities not before they vanish, nor afterwards, but with which they vanish. In like manner the first ratio of nascent quantities is that with which they begin to be. And the first or last sum is that with which they begin and cease to be (or to be augmented or diminished). There is a limit which the velocity at the end of the motion may attain, but not exceed. This is the ultimate velocity. And there is the like limit in all quantities and proportions that begin and cease to be. And since such limits are certain and definite, to determine the same is a problem strictly geometrical. But whatever is geometrical we may be allowed to use in determining and demonstrating any other thing that is likewise geometrical.

It may also be objected, that if the ultimate ratios of evanescent quantities are given, their ultimate magnitudes will be also given: and so all quantities will consist of indivisibles, which is contrary to what Euclid has demonstrated concerning incommensurables, in the 10th Book of his *Elements*. But this objection is founded on a false supposition. For those ultimate ratios with which quantities vanish are not truly the ratios of ultimate quantities, but limits towards which the ratios of quantities decreasing without limit do always converge; and to which they approach nearer than by any given difference, but never go beyond, nor in effect attain to, till the quantities are diminished *in infinitum*. This thing will appear more evident in quantities infinitely great. If two quantities, whose difference is given, be augmented *in infinitum,* the ultimate ratio of these quantities will be given, to wit, the ratio of equality; but it does not from thence follow that the ultimate or greatest quantities themselves, whose ratio that is, will be given. Therefore if in what follows, for the sake of being more easily understood, I should happen to mention quantities as least, or evanescent, or ultimate, you are not to suppose that quantities of any determinate magnitude are meant, but such as are conceived to be always diminished without end.

SECTION TWO

Of the invention of centripetal forces.

PROPOSITION I. THEOREM I.

The areas which revolving bodies describe by radii drawn to an immovable centre of force do lie in the same immovable planes, and are proportional to the times in which they are described.

For suppose the time to be divided into equal parts, and in the first part of that time let the body by its innate force describe the right line AB. In the second part of that time, the same would (by Law I), if not hindered, proceed directly to *c,* along the line B*c* equal to AB; so that by the radii AS, BS, *c*S, drawn to the centre, the equal areas ASB, BS*c,* would be described. But when the body is arrived at B, suppose that a centripetal force acts at once with a great impulse, and, turning aside the body from the right line B*c,* compels it afterwards to continue its motion along the right line BC. Draw *c*C parallel to BS meeting BC in C; and at the end of the second part of the time, the body (by Cor. I of the Laws) will be found in C, in the same plane with the triangle ASB. Join SC, and, because SB and C*c* are parallel, the triangle SBC will be equal to the triangle SB*c,* and therefore also to the triangle SAB. By the like argument, if the centripetal force acts successively in C, D, E, &c., and makes the body, in each single particle of time, to describe the right lines CD, DE, EF, &c., they will all lie in the same plane; and the triangle SCD will be equal to the triangle SBC, and SDE to SCD, and SEF to SDE. And therefore, in equal times, equal areas are described in one immovable plane: and, by composition, any sums SADS, SAFS, of those areas, are one to the other as the times in which they are described. Now let the number of those triangles be augmented, and their breadth diminished *in infinitum;* and (by Cor. IV, Lem. III) their ultimate perimeter ADF will be a curve line: and therefore the centripetal force, by which the body is perpetually drawn back from the tangent of this curve will act continually; and any

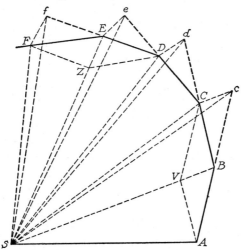

described areas SADS, SAFS, which are always proportional to the times of description, will, in this case also, be proportional to those times. Q.E.D.

Cor. 1. The velocity of a body attracted towards an immovable centre, in spaces void of resistance, is reciprocally as the perpendicular let fall from that centre on the right line that touches the orbit. For the velocities in those places A, B, C, D, E, are as the bases AB, BC, CD, DE, EF, of equal triangles; and these bases are reciprocally as the perpendiculars let fall upon them.

Cor. 2. If the chords AB, BC of two arcs, successively described in equal times by the same body, in spaces void of resistance, are completed into a parallelogram ABCV, and the diagonal BV of this parallelogram, in the position which it ultimately acquires when those arcs are diminished *in infinitum,* is produced both ways, it will pass through the centre of force.

PROPOSITION II. THEOREM II.

Every body that moves in any curve line described in a plane, and by a radius, drawn to a point either immovable, or moving forward with an uniform rectilinear motion, describes about that point areas proportional to the times, is urged by a centripetal force directed to that point.

For every body that moves in a curve line is (by Law I) turned aside from its rectilinear course by the action of some force that impels it. And that force by which the body is turned off from its rectilinear course, and is made to describe, in equal times, the equal least triangles SAB, SBC,

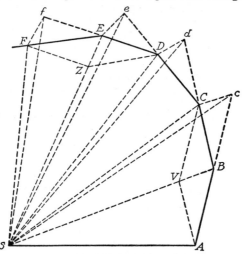

SCD, &c., about the immovable point S (by Prop. XL. Book One, *Elem.* and Law II), acts in the place B, according to the direction of a line parallel to *c*C, that is, in the direction of the line BS, and in the place C, according to the direction of a line parallel to *d*D, that is, in the direction of the line CS, &c.; and therefore acts always in the direction of lines tending to the immovable point S.   Q.E.D.

SCHOLIUM

A body may be urged by a centripetal force compounded of several forces; in which case the meaning of the Proposition is that the force which results out of all tends to the point S. But if any force acts perpetually in the direction of lines perpendicular to the described surface, this force will make the body to deviate from the plane of its motion: but will neither augment nor diminish the quantity of the described surface and is therefore to be neglected in the composition of forces.

PROPOSITION III.   THEOREM III.

Every body that by a radius drawn to the centre of another body, howsoever moved, describes areas about that centre proportional to the times is urged by a force compounded out of the centripetal force

tending to that other body, and of all the accelerative force by which that other body is impelled.

Let L represent the one, and T the other body; and (by Cor. VI of the Laws) if both bodies are urged in the direction of parallel lines, by a new force equal and contrary to that by which the second body T is urged, the first body L will go on to describe about the other body T the same areas as before: but the force by which that other body T was urged will be now destroyed by an equal and contrary force; and therefore (by Law I) that other body T, now left to itself, will either rest or move uniformly forward in a right line: and the first body L, impelled by the difference of the forces, that is, by the force remaining, will go on to describe about the other body T areas proportional to the times. And therefore (by Theor. II) the difference of the forces is directed to the other body T as its centre. Q.E.D.

SCHOLIUM

Because the equable description of areas indicates that a centre is respected by that force with which the body is most affected, and by which it is drawn back from its rectilinear motion, and retained in its orbit; why may we not be allowed, in the following discourse, to use the equable description of areas as an indication of a centre, about which all circular motion is performed in free spaces?

PROPOSITION IV. THEOREM IV.

The centripetal forces of bodies, which by equable motions describe different circles, tend to the centres of the same circles; and are one to the other as the squares of the arcs described in equal times applied to the radii of the circles.

These forces tend to the centres of the circles (by Prop. II and Cor. II, Prop. I), and are one to another as the versed sines of the least arcs described in equal times; that is, as the squares of the same arcs applied to the diameters of the circles (by Lem. VII); and therefore since those arcs are as arcs described in any equal times, and the diameters are as the radii, the forces will be as the squares of any arcs described in the same time applied to the radii of the circles. Q.E.D.

Cor. 1. Therefore, since those arcs are as the velocities of the bodies, the centripetal forces are in a ratio compounded of the duplicate ratio of the velocities directly, and of the simple ratio of the radii inversely.

Cor. 2. And since the periodic times are in a ratio compounded of the ratio of the radii directly and the ratio of the velocities inversely, the centripetal forces are in a ratio compounded of the ratio of the radii directly and the duplicate ratio of the periodic times inversely.

Cor. 3. Whence if the periodic times are equal, and the velocities therefore as the radii, the centripetal forces will be also as the radii; and the contrary.

Cor. 4. If the periodic times and the velocities are both in the subduplicate ratio of the radii, the centripetal forces will be equal among themselves; and the contrary.

Cor. 5. If the periodic times are as the radii, and therefore the velocities equal, the centripetal forces will be reciprocally as the radii; and the contrary.

Cor. 6. If the periodic times are in the sesquiplicate ratio of the radii, and therefore the velocities reciprocally in the subduplicate ratio of the radii, the centripetal forces will be in the duplicate ratio of the radii inversely; and the contrary.

Cor. 7. And universally, if the periodic time is as any power R^n of the radius R, and therefore the velocity reciprocally as the power $R^n{-}^1$ of the radius, the centripetal force will be reciprocally as the power $R^{2n}{-}^1$ of the radius; and the contrary.

Cor. 8. The same things all hold concerning the times, the velocities, and forces by which bodies describe the similar parts of any similar figures that have their centres in a similar position with those figures; as appears by applying the demonstration of the preceding cases to those. And the application is easy, by only substituting the equable description of areas in the place of equable motion, and using the distances of the bodies from the centres instead of the radii.

Cor. 9. From the same demonstration it likewise follows that the arc which a body, uniformly revolving in a circle by means of a given centripetal force, describes in any time is a mean proportional between the diameter of the circle and the space which the same body falling by the same given force would descend through in the same given time.

SCHOLIUM

The case of the 6th Corollary obtains in the celestial bodies (as Sir Christopher Wren, Dr. Hooke, and Dr. Halley have severally observed); and therefore in what follows, I intend to treat more at large of those things which relate to centripetal force decreasing in a duplicate ratio of the distances from the centres.

Moreover, by means of the preceding Proposition and its Corollaries, we may discover the proportion of a centripetal force to any other known force, such as that of gravity. For if a body by means of its gravity revolves in a circle concentric to the earth, this gravity is the centripetal force of that body. But from the descent of heavy bodies, the time of one entire revolution, as well as the arc described in any given time, is given (by Cor. 9 of this Prop.). And by such propositions, Mr. Huygens, in his excellent book *De Horologio Oscillatorio,* has compared the force of gravity with the centrifugal forces of revolving bodies.

The preceding Proposition may be likewise demonstrated after this manner. In any circle suppose a polygon to be inscribed of any number of sides. And if a body, moved with a given velocity along the sides of the polygon, is reflected from the circle at the several angular points, the force, with which at every reflection it strikes the circle, will be as its velocity: and therefore the sum of the forces, in a given time, will be as that velocity and the number of reflections conjunctly; that is (if the species of the polygon be given), as the length described in that given time, and increased or diminished in the ratio of the same length to the radius of the circle; that is, as the square of that length applied to the radius; and therefore the polygon, by having its sides diminished *in infinitum,* coincides with the circle, as the square of the arc described in a given time applied to the radius. This is the centrifugal force, with which the body impels the circle; and to which the contrary force, wherewith the circle continually repels the body towards the centre, is equal.

PROPOSITION V. PROBLEM I.

There being given, in any places, the velocity with which a body describes a given figure, by means of forces directed to some common centre: to find that centre.

Let the three right lines PT, TQV, VR touch the figure described in as many points, P, Q, R, and meet in T and V. On the tangents erect the perpendiculars PA, QB, RC, reciprocally proportional to the veloci-

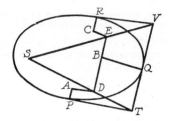

ties of the body in the points P, Q, R, from which the perpendiculars were raised; that is, so that PA may be to QB as the velocity in Q to the velocity in P, and QB to RC as the velocity in R to the velocity in Q. Through the ends A, B, C, of the perpendiculars draw AD, DBE, EC, at right angles, meeting in D and E: and the right lines TD, VE produced, will meet in S, the centre required.

For the perpendiculars let fall from the centre S on the tangents PT, QT, are reciprocally as the velocities of the bodies in the points P and Q (by Cor. I, Prop. I), and therefore, by construction, as the perpendiculars AP, BQ directly; that is, as the perpendiculars let fall from the point D on the tangents. Whence it is easy to infer that the points S, D, T are in one right line. And by the like argument the points S, E, V are also in one right line; and therefore the centre S is in the point where the right lines TD, VE meet.   Q.E.D.

SECTION TWELVE

Of the attractive forces of sphærical bodies.

SCHOLIUM

These Propositions naturally lead us to the analogy there is between centripetal forces, and the central bodies to which those forces used to be directed; for it is reasonable to suppose that forces which are directed to bodies should depend upon the nature and quantity of those bodies, as we see they do in magnetical experiments. And when such cases occur, we are to compute the attractions of the bodies by assigning to each of their particles its proper force, and then collecting the sum of them all. I here use the word attraction in general for any endeavour, of what kind soever, made by bodies to approach to each other; whether that endeavour arise from the action of the bodies themselves, as tending mutually to or agitating each other by spirits emitted; or whether it arises from the action of the æther or of the air, or of any medium whatsoever, whether corporeal or incorporeal, any how impelling bodies placed therein towards each other. In the same general sense I use the word impulse, not defining in this treatise the species or physical qualities of forces, but investigating the quantities and mathematical proportions of them; as I observed before in the Definitions. In mathematics we are to investigate the quantities of forces with their proportions consequent upon any conditions supposed; then, when we enter upon physics, we compare those proportions with the phænomena of Nature, that we may know what conditions of those forces answer to the several kinds of attractive bodies. And this preparation being made, we argue more safely concerning the physical species, causes, and proportions of the forces. Let us see, then, with what forces sphærical bodies consisting of particles endued with attractive powers in the manner above spoken of must act mutually upon one another; and what kind of motions will follow from thence.

PROPOSITION LXX.   THEOREM XXX.

If to every point of a sphærical surface there tend equal centripetal forces decreasing in the duplicate ratio of the distances from those points; I say, that a corpuscle placed within that superficies will not be attracted by those forces any way.

Let HIKL be that sphærical superficies, and P a corpuscle placed within. Through P let there be drawn to this superficies two lines HK, IL, intercepting very small arcs HI, KL; and because (by Cor. 3, Lem. VII) the triangles HPI, LPK are alike, those arcs will be proportional to the distances HP, LP; and any particles at HI and KL of the sphærical superficies, terminated by right lines passing through P, will be in the duplicate ratio of those distances. Therefore the forces of these particles exerted

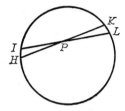

upon the body P are equal between themselves. For the forces are as the particles directly, and the squares of the distances inversely. And these two ratios compose the ratio of equality. The attractions therefore, being made equally towards contrary parts, destroy each other. And by a like reasoning all the attractions through the whole sphærical superficies are destroyed by contrary attractions. Therefore the body P will not be any way impelled by those attractions.   Q.E.D.

PROPOSITION LXXI. THEOREM XXXI.

The same things supposed as above, I say, that a corpuscle placed without the sphærical superficies is attracted towards the centre of the sphere with a force reciprocally proportional to the square of its distance from that centre.

PROPOSITION LXXII. THEOREM XXXII.

If to the several points of a sphere there tend equal centripetal forces decreasing in a duplicate ratio of the distances from those points; and there be given both the density of the sphere and the ratio of the diameter of the sphere to the distance of the corpuscle from its centre; I say, that the force with which the corpuscle is attracted is proportional to the semi-diameter of the sphere.

For conceive two corpuscles to be severally attracted by two spheres, one by one, the other by the other, and their distances from the centres of the spheres to be proportional to the diameters of the spheres respectively, and the spheres to be resolved into like particles, disposed in a like

situation to the corpuscles. Then the attractions of one corpuscle towards
the several particles of one sphere will be to the attractions of the other
towards as many analogous particles of the other sphere in a ratio compounded of the ratio of the particles directly, and the duplicate ratio of
the distances inversely. But the particles are as the spheres, that is, in a
triplicate ratio of the diameters, and the distances are as the diameters;
and the first ratio directly with the last ratio taken twice inversely becomes the ratio of diameter to diameter. Q.E.D.

Cor. 1. Hence if corpuscles revolve in circles about spheres composed
of matter equally attracting, and the distances from the centres of the
spheres be proportional to their diameters, the periodic times will be
equal.

Cor. 2. And, *vice versa,* if the periodic times are equal, the distances
will be proportional to the diameters. These two Corollaries appear from
Cor. 3, Prop. IV.

Cor. 3. If to the several points of any two solids whatever, of like
figure and equal density, there tend equal centripetal forces decreasing in
a duplicate ratio of the distances from those points, the forces, with which
corpuscles placed in a like situation to those two solids will be attracted
by them, will be to each other as the diameters of the solids.

PROPOSITION LXXIII. THEOREM XXXIII.

*If to the several points of a given sphere there tend equal centripetal
forces decreasing in a duplicate ratio of the distances from the point;
I say, that a corpuscle placed within the sphere is attracted by a force
proportional to its distance from the centre.*

In the sphere ABCD, described about the centre S, let there be placed
the corpuscle P; and about the same centre S, with the interval SP, conceive described an interior sphere PEQF. It is plain (by Prop. LXX) that

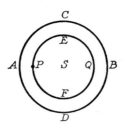

the concentric sphærical superficies, of which the difference AEBF of the
spheres is composed, have no effect at all upon the body P, their attractions being destroyed by contrary attractions. There remains, therefore,
only the attraction of the interior sphere PEQF. And (by Prop. LXXII)
this is as the distance PS. Q.E.D.

SCHOLIUM

By the superficies of which I here imagine the solids composed, I do not mean superficies purely mathematical, but orbs so extremely thin that their thickness is as nothing; that is, the evanescent orbs of which the sphere will at last consist, when the number of the orbs is increased, and their thickness diminished without end. In like manner, by the points of which lines, surfaces, and solids are said to be composed, are to be understood equal particles, whose magnitude is perfectly inconsiderable.

PROPOSITION LXXIV. THEOREM XXXIV.

The same things supposed, I say, that a corpuscle situate without the sphere is attracted with a force reciprocally proportional to the square of its distance from the centre.

For suppose the sphere to be divided into innumerable concentric sphærical superficies, and the attractions of the corpuscle arising from the several superficies will be reciprocally proportional to the square of the distance of the corpuscle from the centre of the sphere (by Prop. LXXI). And, by composition, the sum of those attractions, that is, the attraction of the corpuscle towards the entire sphere, will be in the same ratio. Q.E.D.

Cor. 1. Hence the attractions of homogeneous spheres at equal distances from the centres will be as the spheres themselves. For (by Prop. LXXII) if the distances be proportional to the diameters of the spheres, the forces will be as the diameters. Let the greater distance be diminished in that ratio; and the distances now being equal, the attraction will be increased in the duplicate of that ratio; and therefore will be to the other attraction in the triplicate of that ratio; that is, in the ratio of the spheres.

Cor. 2. At any distances whatever the attractions are as the spheres applied to the squares of the distances.

Cor. 3. If a corpuscle placed without an homogeneous sphere is attracted by a force reciprocally proportional to the square of its distance from the centre, and the sphere consists of attractive particles, the force of every particle will decrease in a duplicate ratio of the distance from each particle.

PROPOSITION LXXV. THEOREM XXXV.

If to the several points of a given sphere there tend equal centripetal forces decreasing in a duplicate ratio of the distances from the point; I say, that another similar sphere will be attracted by it with a force reciprocally proportional to the square of the distance of the centres.

For the attraction of every particle is reciprocally as the square of its distance from the centre of the attracting sphere (by Prop. LXXIV), and is therefore the same as if that whole attracting force issued from one single corpuscle placed in the centre of this sphere. But this attraction is as great as on the other hand the attraction of the same corpuscle would be if that were itself attracted by the several particles of the attracted sphere with the same force with which they are attracted by it. But that attraction of the corpuscle would be (by Prop. LXXIV) reciprocally proportional to the square of its distance from the centre of the sphere; therefore the attraction of the sphere, equal thereto, is also in the same ratio. Q.E.D.

Cor. 1. The attractions of spheres towards other homogeneous spheres are as the attracting spheres applied to the squares of the distances of their centres from the centres of those which they attract.

Cor. 2. The case is the same when the attracted sphere does also attract. For the several points of the one attract the several points of the other with the same force with which they themselves are attracted by the others again; and therefore since in all attractions (by Law III) the attracted and attracting point are both equally acted on, the force will be doubled by their mutual attractions, the proportions remaining.

Cor. 3. Those several truths demonstrated above concerning the motion of bodies about the focus of the conic sections will take place when an attracting sphere is placed in the focus, and the bodies move without the sphere.

Cor. 4. Those things which were demonstrated before of the motion of bodies about the centre of the conic sections take place when the motions are performed within the sphere.

PROPOSITION LXXVI. THEOREM XXXVI.

If spheres be however dissimilar (as to density of matter and attractive force) in the same ratio onward from the centre to the circumference; but every where similar, at every given distance from the centre, on all sides round about; and the attractive force of every point decreases in the duplicate ratio of the distance of the body attracted; I say, that the whole force with which one of these spheres attracts the other will be reciprocally proportional to the square of the distance of the centres.

Imagine several concentric similar spheres, AB, CD, EF, &c., the innermost of which added to the outermost may compose a matter more dense towards the centre, or subducted from them may leave the same more lax and rare. Then, by Prop. LXXV, these spheres will attract other similar concentric spheres GH, IK, LM, &c., each the other, with forces reciprocally proportional to the square of the distance SP. And, by composition or division, the sum of all those forces, or the excess of any of them above the others; that is, the entire force with which the whole sphere AB (composed of any concentric spheres or of their differences) will attract the whole sphere GH (composed of any concentric spheres or their differences) in the same ratio. Let the number of the concentric spheres be increased *in infinitum,* so that the density of the matter together with the attractive force may, in the progress from the circum-

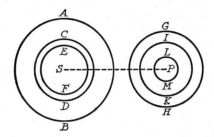

ference to the centre, increase or decrease according to any given law; and by the addition of matter not attractive, let the deficient density be supplied, that so the spheres may acquire any form desired; and the force with which one of these attracts the other will be still, by the former reasoning, in the same ratio of the square of the distance inversely. Q.E.D.

Cor. 1. Hence if many spheres of this kind, similar in all respects, attract each other mutually, the accelerative attractions of each to each, at any equal distances of the centres, will be as the attracting spheres.

Cor. 2. And at any unequal distances, as the attracting spheres applied to the squares of the distances between the centres.

Cor. 3. The motive attractions, or the weights of the spheres towards one another, will be at equal distances of the centres as the attracting and attracted spheres conjunctly; that is, as the products arising from multiplying the spheres into each other.

Cor. 4. And at unequal distances, as those products directly, and the squares of the distances between the centres inversely.

Cor. 5. These proportions take place also when the attraction arises from the attractive virtue of both spheres mutually exerted upon each other. For the attraction is only doubled by the conjunction of the forces, the proportions remaining as before.

Cor. 6. If spheres of this kind revolve about others at rest, each about each; and the distances between the centres of the quiescent and revolving bodies are proportional to the diameters of the quiescent bodies; the periodic times will be equal.

Cor 7. And, again, if the periodic times are equal, the distances will be proportional to the diameters.

Cor. 8. All those truths above demonstrated, relating to the motions of bodies about the foci of conic sections, will take place when an attracting sphere, of any form and condition like that above described, is placed in the focus.

Cor. 9. And also when the revolving bodies are also attracting spheres of any condition like that above described.

PROPOSITION LXXVII.   THEOREM XXXVII.

If to the several points of spheres there tend centripetal forces proportional to the distances of the points from the attracted bodies; I say, that the compounded force with which two spheres attract each other mutually is as the distance between the centres of the spheres.

PROPOSITION LXXVIII.   THEOREM XXXVIII.

If spheres in the progress from the centre to the circumference be however dissimilar and unequable, but similar on every side round about at all given distances from the centre; and the attractive force of every point be as the distance of the attracted body; I say, that the entire force with which two spheres of this kind attract each other mutually is proportional to the distance between the centres of the spheres.

SCHOLIUM

I have now explained the two principal cases of attractions; to wit, when the centripetal forces decrease in a duplicate ratio of the distances, or increase in a simple ratio of the distances, causing the bodies in both cases to revolve in conic sections, and composing sphærical bodies whose centripetal forces observe the same law of increase or decrease in the recess from the centre as the forces or the particles themselves do; which is very remarkable. It would be tedious to run over the other cases, whose conclusions are less elegant and important, so particularly as I have done these.

Book Two: Of the Motion of Bodies

SECTION SIX

Of the motion and resistance of funependulous bodies

PROPOSITION XXIV. THEOREM XIX.

The quantities of matter in funependulous bodies, whose centres of oscillation are equally distant from the centre of suspension, are in a ratio compounded of the ratio of the weights and the duplicate ratio of the times of the oscillations in vacuo.

For the velocity which a given force can generate in a given matter in a given time is as the force and the time directly, and the matter inversely. The greater the force or the time is, or the less the matter, the greater velocity will be generated. This is manifest from the second Law of Motion. Now if pendulums are of the same length, the motive forces in places equally distant from the perpendicular are as the weights: and therefore if two bodies by oscillating describe equal arcs, and those arcs are divided into equal parts; since the times in which the bodies describe each of the correspondent parts of the arcs are as the times of the whole oscillations, the velocities in the correspondent parts of the oscillations will be to each other as the motive forces and the whole times of the oscillations directly, and the quantities of matter reciprocally: and therefore the quantities of matter are as the forces and the times of the oscillations directly and the velocities reciprocally. But the velocities reciprocally are as the times, and therefore the times directly and the velocities reciprocally are as the squares of the times; and therefore the quantities of matter are as the motive forces and the squares of the times, that is, as the weights and the squares of the times.   Q.E.D.

Cor. 1. Therefore if the times are equal, the quantities of matter in each of the bodies are as the weights.

Cor. 2. If the weights are equal, the quantities of matter will be as the squares of the times.

Cor. 3. If the quantities of matter are equal, the weights will be reciprocally as the squares of the times.

Cor. 4. Whence since the squares of the times, *cæteris paribus,* are as the lengths of the pendulums, therefore if both the times and quantities of matter are equal, the weights will be as the lengths of the pendulums.

Cor. 5. And universally, the quantity of matter in the pendulous body is as the square of the time directly, and the length of the pendulum inversely.

Cor. 6. But in a non-resisting medium, the quantity of matter in the pendulous body is as the comparative weight and the square of the time directly, and the length of the pendulum inversely. For the comparative weight is the motive force of the body in any heavy medium, as was shown above; and therefore does the same thing in such a non-resisting medium as the absolute weight does in a vacuum.

Cor. 7. And hence appears a method both of comparing bodies one among another, as to the quantity of matter in each; and of comparing the weights of the same body in different places, to know the variation of its gravity. And by experiments made with the greatest accuracy, I have always found the quantity of matter in bodies to be proportional to their weight.

Book Three: Natural Philosophy

IN THE preceding Books I have laid down the principles of philosophy, principles not philosophical, but mathematical: such, to wit, as we may build our reasonings upon in philosophical inquiries. These principles are the laws and conditions of certain motions, and powers or forces, which chiefly have respect to philosophy; but, lest they should have appeared of themselves dry and barren, I have illustrated them here and there with some philosophical scholiums, giving an account of such things as are of more general nature, and which philosophy seems chiefly to be founded on; such as the density and the resistance of bodies, spaces void of all bodies, and the motion of light and sounds. It remains that, from the same principles, I now demonstrate the frame of the System of the World. Upon this subject I had, indeed, composed the third Book in a popular method, that it might be read by many; but afterward, considering that such as had not sufficiently entered into the principles could not easily discern the strength of the consequences, nor lay aside the prejudices to which they had been many years accustomed, therefore, to prevent the disputes which might be raised upon such accounts, I chose to reduce the substance of this Book into the form of Propositions (in the mathematical way), which should be read by those only who had first made themselves masters of the principles established in the preceding Books.

RULES OF REASONING IN PHILOSOPHY

RULE I

We are to admit no more causes of natural things than such as are both true and sufficient to explain their appearances.

To this purpose the philosophers say that Nature does nothing in vain, and more is in vain when less will serve; for Nature is pleased with simplicity, and affects not the pomp of superfluous causes.

RULE II

Therefore to the same natural effects we must, as far as possible, assign the same causes.

As to respiration in a man and in a beast; the descent of stones in *Europe* and in *America;* the light of our culinary fire and of the sun; the reflection of light in the earth, and in the planets.

RULE III

The qualities of bodies, which admit neither intension nor remission of degrees, and which are found to belong to all bodies within the reach of our experiments, are to be esteemed the universal qualities of all bodies whatsoever.

For since the qualities of bodies are only known to us by experiments, we are to hold for universal all such as universally agree with experiments; and such as are not liable to diminution can never be quite taken away. We are certainly not to relinquish the evidence of experiments for the sake of dreams and vain fictions of our own devising; nor are we to recede from the analogy of Nature, which uses to be simple, and always consonant to itself. We no other way know the extension of bodies than by our senses, nor do these reach it in all bodies; but because we perceive extension in all that are sensible, therefore we ascribe it universally to all others also. That abundance of bodies are hard, we learn by experience; and because the hardness of the whole arises from the hardness of the parts, we therefore justly infer the hardness of the undivided particles not only of the bodies we feel but of all others. That all bodies are impenetrable, we gather not from reason, but from sensation. The bodies which we handle we find impenetrable, and thence conclude impenetrability to be an universal property of all bodies whatsoever. That all bodies are movable, and endowed with certain powers (which we call the *vires inertiæ*) of persevering in their motion, or in their rest, we only infer from the like properties observed in the bodies which we have seen. The extension, hardness, impenetrability, mobility, and *vis inertiæ* of the whole, result from the extension, hardness, impenetrability, mobility, and *vires inertiæ* of the parts; and thence we conclude the least particles of all bodies to be also all extended, and hard and impenetrable, and movable, and endowed with their proper *vires inertiæ*. And this is the foundation of all philosophy. Moreover, that the divided but contiguous particles of bodies may be separated from one another is matter of observation; and, in the particles that remain undivided, our minds are able to distinguish yet lesser parts, as is mathematically demonstrated. But whether the parts so distinguished, and not yet divided, may, by the powers of Nature, be actually divided and separated from one another, we cannot certainly determine. Yet, had we the proof of but one experiment that any undivided particle, in breaking a hard and solid body, suffered a division, we might by virtue of this rule conclude that the undivided as well as the divided particles may be divided and actually separated to infinity.

Lastly, if it universally appears, by experiments and astronomical observations, that all bodies about the earth gravitate towards the earth, and that in proportion to the quantity of matter which they severally contain; that the moon likewise, according to the quantity of its matter, gravitates towards the earth; that, on the other hand, our sea gravitates towards the moon; and all the planets mutually one towards another; and the comets in like manner towards the sun; we must, in consequence of this rule, universally allow that all bodies whatsoever are endowed with a principle of mutual gravitation. For the argument from the appearances concludes with more force for the universal gravitation of all bodies than for their impenetrability; of which, among those in the celestial regions, we have no experiments, nor any manner of observation. Not that I affirm gravity to be essential to bodies: by their *vis insita* I mean nothing but their *vis inertiæ*. This is immutable. Their gravity is diminished as they recede from the earth.

RULE IV

In experimental philosophy we are to look upon propositions collected by general induction from phænomena as accurately or very nearly true, notwithstanding any contrary hypotheses that may be imagined, till such time as other phænomena occur, by which they may either be made more accurate or liable to exceptions.

This rule we must follow, that the argument of induction may not be evaded by hypotheses.

PHÆNOMENA, OR APPEARANCES

PHÆNOMENON I

That the circumjovial planets, by radii drawn to Jupiter's centre, describe areas proportional to the times of description; and that their periodic times, the fixed stars being at rest, are in the sesquiplicate proportion of their distances from its centre.

This we know from astronomical observations. For the orbits of these planets differ but insensibly from circles concentric to Jupiter; and their motions in those circles are found to be uniform. And all astronomers agree that their periodic times are in the sesquiplicate proportion of the semi-diameters of their orbits; and so it manifestly appears from the following table.

The periodic times of the satellites of Jupiter.

1^d. 18^h. $27'$ $34''$. 3^d. 13^h. $13'$ $42''$. 7^d. 3^h. $42'$ $36''$. 16^d. 16^h. $32'$ $9''$.

The distances of the satellites from Jupiter's centre.

From the observations of	1	2	3	4	
Borelli	$5\frac{2}{3}$	$8\frac{2}{3}$	14	$24\frac{2}{3}$	semi-diameter of Jupiter
Townly *by the Microm.* . .	5,52	8,78	13,47	24,72	
Cassini *by the Telescope* . .	5	8	13	23	
Cassini *by the eclip. of the satel.*	$5\frac{2}{3}$	9	$14^{23}\!/_{60}$	$25^{3}\!/_{10}$	
From the periodic times	5,667	9,017	14,384	25,299	

PHÆNOMENON II

That the circumsaturnal planets, by radii drawn to Saturn's centre, describe areas proportional to the times of description; and that their periodic times, the fixed stars being at rest, are in the sesquiplicate proportion of their distances from its centre.

PHÆNOMENON III

That the five primary planets, Mercury, Venus, Mars, Jupiter, and Saturn, with their several orbits, encompass the sun.

That Mercury and Venus revolve about the sun is evident from their moon-like appearances. When they shine out with a full face, they are, in respect of us, beyond or above the sun; when they appear half full, they are about the same height on one side or other of the sun; when horned, they are below or between us and the sun; and they are sometimes, *when directly under,* seen like spots traversing the sun's disk. That Mars surrounds the sun is as plain from its full face when near its conjunction with the sun, and from the gibbous figure which it shews in its quadratures. And the same thing is demonstrable of Jupiter and Saturn, from their appearing full in all situations; for the shadows of their satellites that appear sometimes upon their disks make it plain that the light they shine with is not their own, but borrowed from the sun.

PHÆNOMENON IV

That the fixed stars being at rest, the periodic times of the five primary planets, and (whether of the sun about the earth, or) of the earth about the sun, are in the sesquiplicate proportion of their mean distances from the sun.

This proportion, first observed by *Kepler,* is now received by all astronomers; for the periodic times are the same, and the dimensions of the orbits are the same, whether the sun revolves about the earth, or the earth about the sun. And as to the measures of the periodic times, all astronomers are agreed about them.

PHÆNOMENON V

Then the primary planets, by radii drawn to the earth, describe areas no wise proportional to the times; but that the areas which they describe by radii drawn to the sun are proportional to the times of description.

For to the earth they appear sometimes direct, sometimes stationary, nay, and sometimes retrograde. But from the sun they are always seen direct, and to proceed with a motion nearly uniform, that is to say, a little swifter in the perihelion and a little slower in the aphelion distances, so as to maintain an equality in the description of the areas. This a noted proposition among astronomers, and particularly demonstrable in Jupiter, from the eclipses of his satellites; by the help of which eclipses, as we have said, the heliocentric longitudes of that planet, and its distances from the sun, are determined.

PHÆNOMENON VI

That the moon, by a radius drawn to the earth's centre, describes an area proportional to the time of description.

This we gather from the apparent motion of the moon, compared with its apparent diameter. It is true that the motion of the moon is a little disturbed by the action of the sun: but in laying down these Phænomena, I neglect those small and inconsiderable errors.

PROPOSITIONS

PROPOSITION I.   THEOREM I.

That the forces by which the circumjovial planets are continually drawn off from rectilinear motions, and retained in their proper orbits, tend to Jupiter's centre; and are reciprocally as the squares of the distances of the places of those planets from that centre.

The former part of this Proposition appears from Phæn. I and Prop. II or III, Book One; the latter from Phæn. I and Cor. 6, Prop. IV, of the same Book.

The same thing we are to understand of the planets which encompass Saturn, by Phæn. II.

PROPOSITION II. THEOREM II.

That the forces by which the primary planets are continually drawn off from rectilinear motions, and retained in their proper orbits, tend to the sun; and are reciprocally as the squares of the distances of the places of those planets from the sun's centre.

The former part of the Proposition is manifest from Phæn. V and Prop. II, Book One; the latter from Phæn. IV and Cor. 6, Prop. IV, of the same Book. But this part of the Proposition is, with great accuracy, demonstrable from the quiescence of the aphelion points; for a very small aberration from the *reciprocal* duplicate proportion would produce a motion of the apsides sensible enough in every single revolution, and in many of them enormously great.

PROPOSITION III. THEOREM III.

That the force by which the moon is retained in its orbit tends to the earth; and is reciprocally as the square of the distance of its place from the earth's centre.

The former part of the Proposition is evident from Phæn. VI and Prop. II or III, Book One; the latter from the very slow motion of the moon's apogee; which in every single revolution amounting but to 3° 3′ *in consequentia,* may be neglected.

PROPOSITION IV. THEOREM IV.

That the moon gravitates towards the earth, and by the force of gravity is continually drawn off from a rectilinear motion, and retained in its orbit.

The mean distance of the moon from the earth in the syzygies in semi-diameters of the earth is, according to *Ptolemy* and most astronomers, 59; according to *Vendelin* and *Huygens,* 60; to *Copernicus,* 60⅓; to *Street,* 60⅖; and to *Tycho,* 56½. But *Tycho,* and all that follow his tables of refraction, making the refractions of the sun and moon (altogether against the nature of light) to exceed the refractions of the fixed stars, and that by four or five minutes *near the horizon,* did thereby increase the moon's *horizontal* parallax by a like number of minutes, that is, by a twelfth or fifteenth part of the whole parallax. Correct this error, and the distance will become about 60½ semi-diameters of the earth, near to what others have assigned. Let us assume the mean distance of 60 diameters in the syzygies; and suppose one revolution of the moon, in respect of the fixed stars, to be completed in 27^d. 7^h. 43′, as astronomers have determined; and the circumference of the earth to amount to 123249600 *Paris* feet, as the French have found by mensuration. And now if we imagine the moon, deprived of all motion, to be let go, so as to descend towards the earth with the impulse of all that force by which (by Prop. III) it is retained in its orb, it will in the space of one minute of time, describe in its fall $15\frac{1}{12}$ *Paris* feet. This we gather by a calculus, founded upon Cor. 9, Prop. IV, of the same Book. For the versed sine of that arc, which the moon, in the space of one minute of time, would by its mean motion describe at the distance of 60 semi-diameters of the earth, is nearly $15\frac{1}{12}$ *Paris* feet, or more accurately 15 feet, 1 inch, and 1 line $\frac{4}{9}$. Wherefore, since that force, in approaching to the earth, increases in the reciprocal duplicate proportion of the distance, and, upon that account, at the surface of the earth, is 60×60 times greater than at the moon, a body in our regions, falling with that force, ought, in the space of one minute of time, to describe $60\times60\times15\frac{1}{12}$ *Paris* feet; and, in the space of one second of time, to describe $15\frac{1}{12}$ of those feet; or, more accurately, 15 feet, 1 inch, and 1 line $\frac{4}{9}$. And with this very force we actually find that bodies here upon earth do really descend; for a pendulum oscillating seconds in the latitude of *Paris* will be 3 *Paris* feet, and 8 lines $\frac{1}{2}$ in length, as Mr. *Huygens* has observed. And the space which a heavy body describes by falling in one second of time is to half the length of this pendulum in the duplicate ratio of the circumference of a circle to its diameter (as Mr. *Huygens* has also shewn), and is therefore 15 *Paris* feet, 1 inch, 1 line $\frac{7}{9}$. And therefore the force by which the moon is retained in its orbit becomes, at the very surface of the earth, equal to the force of gravity which we observe in heavy bodies there. And therefore (by Rule I and II) the force by which the moon is retained in its orbit is that very same force which we commonly call gravity; for, were gravity another force different from that, then bodies descending to the earth with the joint impulse of both forces would fall with a double velocity, and in the space of one second of time would describe $30\frac{1}{6}$ *Paris* feet; altogether against experience.

This calculus is founded on the hypothesis of the earth's standing still; for if both earth and moon move about the sun, and at the same time about their common centre of gravity, the distance of the centres of the moon and earth from one another will be $60\frac{1}{2}$ semi-diameters of the earth.

SCHOLIUM

The demonstration of this Proposition may be more diffusely explained after the following manner. Suppose several moons to revolve about the earth, as in the system of Jupiter or Saturn; the periodic times of these moons (by the argument of induction) would observe the same law which *Kepler* found to obtain among the planets; and therefore their centripetal forces would be reciprocally as the squares of the distances from the centre of the earth, by Prop. I of this Book. Now if the lowest of these were very small, and were so near the earth as almost to touch the tops of the highest mountains, the centripetal force thereof, retaining it in its orb, would be very nearly equal to the weights of any *terrestrial* bodies that should be found upon the tops of those mountains, as may be known by the foregoing computation. Therefore if the same little moon should be deserted by its centrifugal force that carries it through its orb, and so be disabled from going onward therein, it would descend to the earth; and that with the same velocity as heavy bodies do actually fall with upon the tops of those very mountains; because of the equality of the forces that oblige them both to descend. And if the force by which that lowest moon would descend were different from gravity, and if that moon were to gravitate towards the earth, as we find terrestrial bodies do upon the tops of mountains, it would then descend with twice the velocity, as being impelled by both these forces conspiring together. Therefore since both these forces, that is, the gravity of heavy bodies, and the centripetal forces of the moons, respect the centre of the earth, and are similar and equal between themselves, they will (by Rule I and II) have one and the same cause. And therefore the force which retains the moon in its orbit is that very force which we commonly call gravity; because otherwise this little moon at the top of a mountain must either be without gravity or fall twice as swiftly as heavy bodies are wont to do.

PROPOSITION V. THEOREM V.

That the circumjovial planets gravitate towards Jupiter; the circumsa-turnal towards Saturn; the circumsolar towards the sun; and by the forces of their gravity are drawn off from rectilinear motions, and retained in curvilinear orbits.

Cor. 1. There is, therefore, a power of gravity tending to all the planets; for, doubtless, Venus, Mercury, and the rest, are bodies of the same sort with Jupiter and Saturn. And since all attraction (by Law III) is mutual, Jupiter will therefore gravitate towards all his own satellites, Saturn towards his, the earth towards the moon, and the sun towards all the primary planets.

Cor. 2. The force of gravity which tends to any one planet is re-ciprocally as the square of the distance of places from that planet's centre.

Cor. 3. All the planets do mutually gravitate towards one another, by Cor. 1 and 2. And hence it is that Jupiter and Saturn, when near their conjunction, by their mutual attractions sensibly disturb each other's motions. So the sun disturbs the motions of the moon; and both sun and moon disturb our sea, as we shall hereafter explain.

SCHOLIUM

The force which retains the celestial bodies in their orbits has been hitherto called centripetal force; but it being now made plain that it can be no other than a gravitating force, we shall hereafter call it gravity. For the cause of that centripetal force which retains the moon in its orbit will extend itself to all the planets, by Rules I, II, and IV.

PROPOSITION VI.   THEOREM VI.

That all bodies gravitate towards every planet; and that the weights of bodies towards any the same planet, at equal distances from the centre of the planet, are proportional to the quantities of matter which they severally contain.

It has been, now of a long time, observed by others that all sorts of heavy bodies (allowance being made for the inequality of retardation which they suffer from a small power of resistance in the air) descend to the earth *from equal heights* in equal times; and that equality of times we may distinguish to a great accuracy, by the help of pendulums. I tried the thing in gold, silver, lead, glass, sand, common salt, wood, water, and wheat. I provided two wooden boxes, round and equal: I filled the one with wood, and suspended an equal weight of gold (as exactly as I could) in the centre of oscillation of the other. The boxes hanging by equal threads of 11 feet made a couple of pendulums perfectly equal in weight and figure, and equally receiving the resistance of the air. And, placing the one by the other, I observed them to play together forward and backward, for a long time, with equal vibrations. And therefore the quantity of matter in the gold (by Cor. 1 and 6, Prop. XXIV, Book Two) was to the quantity of matter in the wood as the action of the motive force (or *vis motrix*) upon all the gold to the action of the same upon all the wood; that is, as the weight of the one to the weight of the other: and the like happened in the other bodies. By these experiments, in bodies of the same weight, I could manifestly have discovered a difference of matter less than the thousandth part of the whole, had any such been. But, without all doubt, the nature of gravity towards the planets is the same as towards the earth. For, should we imagine our terrestrial bodies removed to the orb of the moon, and there, together with the moon, deprived of all motion, to be let go, so as to fall together towards the earth, it is certain, from what we have demonstrated before, that, in equal times, they would describe equal spaces with the moon, and of consequence are to the moon, in quantity of matter, as their weights to its weight. Moreover, since the satellites of Jupiter perform their revolutions in times which observe the sesquiplicate proportion of their distances from Jupiter's centre, their accelerative gravities towards Jupiter will be reciprocally as the squares of their distances from Jupiter's centre; that is, equal, at equal distances. And, therefore, these satellites, if supposed to fall *towards Jupiter* from equal heights, would describe equal spaces in equal times, in like manner as heavy bodies do on our earth. And, by the same argument, if the circumsolar planets were supposed to be let fall at equal distances from the sun, they would, in their descent towards the sun, describe equal spaces in equal times. But forces which equally accelerate unequal bodies must be as those bodies: that is to say, the weights of the planets *towards the sun* must be as their quantities of matter. Further, that the weights of Jupiter and of his satellites towards the sun are proportional to the several quantities of their matter appears from the exceedingly regular motions of the satellites. For if some of those bodies were more strongly attracted to the sun in proportion to their quantity of matter than others, the motions of the satellites would be disturbed by that inequality of attraction. If, at equal distances from the sun, any satellite, in proportion to the quantity of its matter, did gravitate towards the sun with a force greater than Jupiter in proportion to his, according to any given proportion, suppose of d to e; then the distance between the centres of the sun and of the satellite's orbit would be always greater than the distance between the centres of the sun and of Jupiter nearly in the subduplicate of that proportion: as by some computations I have found. And if the satellite did gravitate towards the sun with a force, lesser in the proportion of e to d, the distance of the centre of the satellite's orb from the sun would be less than the distance of the centre of Jupiter from the sun in the subduplicate of the same proportion. Therefore if, at equal distances from the sun, the accelerative gravity of any satellite towards the sun were greater or less than the accelerative gravity of Jupiter towards the sun but by one $\frac{1}{1000}$ part of the whole gravity, the distance of the centre of the satellite's orbit from the sun would be greater or less than the distance of Jupiter from the sun by one $\frac{1}{2000}$ part of the whole distance; that is, by a fifth part of the distance of the utmost satellite from the centre of Jupiter; an eccentricity of the orbit which would be very sensible. But the orbits of the satellites are concentric to Jupiter, and therefore the accelerative gravities of Jupiter, and of all its satellites towards the sun, are equal among themselves. And by the same argument, the weights of Saturn and of his satellites towards the sun, at equal distances from the sun, are as their several quantities of matter; and the weights of the moon and of the earth towards the sun are either none, or accurately proportional to the masses of matter which they contain. But some they are, by Cor. 1 and 3, Prop. V.

But further; the weights of all the parts of every planet towards any other planet are one to another as the matter in the several parts; for if some parts did gravitate more, others less, than for the quantity of their matter, then the whole planet, according to the sort of parts with which it most abounds, would gravitate more or less than in proportion to the quantity of matter in the whole. Nor is it of any moment whether these parts are external or internal; for if, for example, we should imagine the terrestrial bodies with us to be raised up to the orb of the moon, to be there compared with its body: if the weights of such bodies were to the weights of the external parts of the moon as the quantities of matter in the one and in the other respectively; but to the weights of the internal parts in a greater or less proportion, then likewise the weights of those bodies would be to the weight of the whole moon in a greater or less proportion; against what we have shewed above.

Cor. 1. Hence the weights of bodies do not depend upon their forms and textures; for if the weights could be altered with the forms, they would be greater or less, according to the variety of forms, in equal matter; altogether against experience.

Cor. 2. Universally, all bodies about the earth gravitate towards the earth; and the weights of all, at equal distances from the earth's centre, are as the quantities of matter which they severally contain. This is the quality of all bodies within the reach of our experiments; and therefore (by Rule III) to be affirmed of all bodies whatsoever.

Cor. 3. All spaces are not equally full; for if all spaces were equally full, then the specific gravity of the fluid which fills the region of the air, on account of the extreme density of the matter, would fall nothing short of the specific gravity of quicksilver, or gold, or any other the most dense body; and, therefore, neither gold, nor any other body, could descend in air; for bodies do not descend in fluids, unless they are specifically heavier than the fluids. And if the quantity of matter in a given space can, by any rarefaction, be diminished, what should hinder a diminution to infinity?

Cor. 4. If all the solid particles of all bodies are of the same density, nor can be rarefied without pores, a void, space, or vacuum must be granted. By bodies of the same density, I mean those whose *vires inertiæ* are in the proportion of their bulks.

Cor. 5. The power of gravity is of a different nature from the power of magnetism; for the magnetic attraction is not as the matter attracted. Some bodies are attracted more by the magnet; others less; most bodies not at all. The power of magnetism in one and the same body may be increased and diminished; and is sometimes far stronger, for the quantity of matter, than the power of gravity; and in receding from the magnet decreases not in the duplicate but almost in the triplicate proportion of the distance, as nearly as I could judge from some rude observations.

PROPOSITION VII.　THEOREM VII.

That there is a power of gravity tending to all bodies, proportional to the several quantities of matter which they contain.

That all the planets mutually gravitate one towards another, we have proved before; as well as that the force of gravity towards every one of them, considered apart, is reciprocally as the square of the distance of places from the centre of the planet. And thence it follows that the gravity tending towards all the planets is proportional to the matter which they contain.

Moreover, since all the parts of any planet A gravitate towards any other planet B; and the gravity of every part is to the gravity of the whole as the matter of the part to the matter of the whole; and (by Law III) to every action corresponds an equal re-action; therefore the planet B will, on the other hand, gravitate towards all the parts of the planet A;

and its gravity towards any one part will be to the gravity towards the whole as the matter of the part to the matter of the whole. Q.E.D.

COR. 1. Therefore the force of gravity towards any whole planet arises from, and is compounded of, the forces of gravity towards all its parts. Magnetic and electric attractions afford us examples of this; for all attraction towards the whole arises from the attractions towards the several parts. The thing may be easily understood in gravity, if we consider a greater planet, as formed of a number of lesser planets, meeting together in one globe; for *hence it would appear that* the force of the whole must arise from the forces of the component parts. If it is objected, that, according to this law, all bodies with us must mutually gravitate one towards another, whereas no such gravitation any where appears, I answer, that since the gravitation towards these bodies is to the gravitation towards the whole earth as these bodies are to the whole earth, the gravitation towards them must be far less than to fall under the observation of our senses.

COR. 2. The force of gravity towards the several equal particles of any body is reciprocally as the square of the distance of places from the particles; as appears from Cor. 3, Prop. LXXIV, Book One.

PROPOSITION VIII. THEOREM VIII.

In two spheres mutually gravitating each towards the other, if the matter in places on all sides round about and equidistant from the centres is similar, the weight of either sphere towards the other will be reciprocally as the square of the distance between their centres.

After I had found that the force of gravity towards a whole planet did arise from and was compounded of the forces of gravity towards all its parts, and towards every one part was in the reciprocal proportion of the squares of the distances from the part, I was yet in doubt whether that reciprocal duplicate proportion did accurately hold, or but nearly so, in the total force compounded of so many partial ones; for it might be that the proportion which accurately enough took place in greater distances should be wide of the truth near the surface of the planet, where the distances of the particles are unequal, and their situation dissimilar. But by the help of Prop. LXXV and LXXVI, Book One, and their Corollaries, I was at last satisfied of the truth of the Proposition, as it now lies before us.

COR. 1. Hence we may find and compare together the weights of bodies towards different planets; for the weights of bodies revolving in circles about planets are (by Cor. 2, Prop. IV, Book One) as the diameters of the circles directly, and the squares of their periodic times reciprocally; and their weights at the surfaces of the planets, or at any other distances from their centres, are (by this Prop.) greater or less in the reciprocal duplicate proportion of the distances. Thus from the periodic times of Venus, revolving about the sun, in $224^d. 16\frac{3}{4}^h$, of the utmost circumjovial satellite revolving about Jupiter, in $16^d. 16\frac{8}{15}^h$.; of the Huygenian satellite about Saturn in 15^d. $22\frac{2}{3}^h$.; and of the moon about the earth in 27^d. 7^h. $43'$; compared with the mean distance of Venus from the sun, and with the greatest heliocentric elongations of the outmost circumjovial satellite from Jupiter's centre, $8'\ 16''$; of the Huygenian satellite from the centre of Saturn, $3'\ 4''$; and of the moon from the earth, $10'\ 33''$: by computation I found that the weight of equal bodies, at equal distances from the centres of the sun, of Jupiter, of Saturn, and of the earth, towards the sun, Jupiter, Saturn, and the earth, were one to another, as 1, $\frac{1}{1067}$, $\frac{1}{3021}$, and $\frac{1}{169282}$ respectively. Then because as the distances are increased or diminished, the weights are diminished or increased in a duplicate ratio, the weights of equal bodies towards the sun, Jupiter, Saturn, and the earth, at the distances 10000, 997, 791, and 109 from their centres, that is, at their very superficies, will be as 10000, 943, 529, and 435 respectively. How much the weights of bodies are at the superficies of the moon will be shewn hereafter.

Cor. 2. Hence likewise we discover the quantity of matter in the several planets; for their quantities of matter are as the forces of gravity at equal distances from their centres; that is, in the sun, Jupiter, Saturn, and the earth, as 1, $\frac{1}{1067}$, $\frac{1}{3021}$, and $\frac{1}{169282}$ respectively. If the parallax of the sun be taken greater or less than $10''\ 30'''$, the quantity of matter in the earth must be augmented or diminished in the triplicate of that proportion.

Cor. 3. Hence also we find the densities of the planets; for (by Prop. LXXII, Book One) the weights of equal and similar bodies towards similar spheres are, at the surfaces of those spheres, as the diameters of the spheres; and therefore the densities of dissimilar spheres are as those weights applied to the diameters of the spheres. But the true diameters of the sun, Jupiter, Saturn, and the earth were one to another as 10000, 997, 791, and 109; and the weights towards the same as 10000, 943, 529, and 435 respectively; and therefore their densities are as 100, $94\frac{1}{2}$, 67, and 400. The density of the earth, which comes out by this computation, does not depend upon the parallax of the sun, but is determined by the parallax of the moon, and therefore is here truly defined. The sun, therefore, is a little denser than Jupiter, and Jupiter than Saturn, and the earth four times denser than the sun; for the sun, by its great heat, is kept in a sort of a rarefied state. The moon is denser than the earth, as shall appear afterward.

Cor. 4. The smaller the planets are, they are, *cæteris paribus*, of so much the greater density; for so the powers of gravity on their several surfaces come nearer to equality. They are likewise, *cæteris paribus*, of the greater density, as they are nearer to the sun. So Jupiter is more dense than Saturn, and the earth than Jupiter; for the planets were to be placed at different distances from the sun, that, according to their, degrees of density, they might enjoy a greater or less proportion to the sun's heat. Our water, if it were removed as far as the orb of Saturn, would be converted into ice, and in the orb of Mercury would quickly fly away in vapour; for the light of the sun, to which its heat is proportional, is seven times denser in the orb of Mercury than with us: and by the thermometer I have found that a sevenfold heat of our summer sun will make water boil. Nor are we to doubt that the matter of Mercury is adapted to its heat, and is therefore more dense than the matter of our earth; since, in a denser matter, the operations of Nature require a stronger heat.

PROPOSITION IX. THEOREM IX.

That the force of gravity, considered downward from the surface of the planets, decreases nearly in the proportion of the distances from their centres.

PROPOSITION X. THEOREM X.

That the motions of the planets in the heavens may subsist an exceedingly long time.

I have shewed that a globe of water frozen into ice, and moving freely in our air, in the time that it would describe the length of its semi-diameter, would lose by the resistance of the air $\frac{1}{4586}$ part of its motion; and the same proportion holds nearly in all globes, how great soever, and moved with whatever velocity. But that our globe of earth is of greater density than it would be if the whole consisted of water only, I thus make out. If the whole consisted of water only, whatever was of less density than water, because of its less specific gravity, would emerge and float above. And upon this account, if a globe of terrestrial matter, covered on all sides with water, was less dense than water, it would emerge somewhere; and, the subsiding water falling back, would be gathered to the opposite side. And such is the condition of our earth, which in a great measure is covered with seas. The earth, if it was not for its greater density, would emerge from the seas, and, according to its degree of levity, would be raised more or less above their surface, the water of the seas flowing backward to the opposite side. By the same argument, the spots of the sun, which float upon the lucid matter thereof, are lighter than that matter; and, however the planets have been formed while they were yet in fluid masses, all the heavier matter subsided to the centre. Since, therefore, the common matter of our earth on the surface thereof is about twice as heavy as water, and a little lower, in mines, is found about three, or four, or even five times more heavy, it is probable that the quantity of the whole matter of the earth may be five or six times greater than if it consisted all of water; especially since I have before shewed that the earth is about four times more dense than Jupiter. If, therefore, Jupiter is a little more dense than water, in the space of thirty days, in which that planet describes the length of 459 of its semi-diameters, it would, in a medium of the same density with our air, lose almost a tenth part of its motion. But since the resistance of mediums decreases in proportion to their weight or density, so that water, which is $13\frac{3}{5}$ times lighter than quicksilver, resists less in that proportion; and air, which is 860 times lighter than water, resists less in the same proportion; therefore in the heavens, where the weight of the medium in which the planets move is immensely diminished, the resistance will almost vanish.

It is shewn that at the height of 200 miles above the earth the air is more rare than it is at the superficies of the earth in the ratio of 30 to 0,0000000000003998, or as 75000000000000 to 1 nearly. And hence the planet Jupiter, revolving in a medium of the same density with that superior air, would not lose by the resistance of the medium the 1000000th part of its motion in 1000000 years. In the spaces near the earth the resistance is produced only by the air, exhalations, and vapours. When these are carefully exhausted by the air pump from under the receiver, heavy bodies fall within the receiver with perfect freedom, and without the least sensible resistance: gold itself, and the lightest down, let fall together, will descend with equal velocity; and though they fall through a space of four, six, and eight feet, they will come to the bottom at the same time; as appears from experiments. And therefore the celestial regions being perfectly void of air and exhalations, the planets and comets meeting no sensible resistance in those spaces will continue their motions through them for an immense tract of time.

HYPOTHESIS I

That the centre of the system of the world is immovable.

This is acknowledged by all, while some contend that the earth, others that the sun, is fixed in that center. Let us see what may from hence follow.

PROPOSITION XI.   THEOREM XI.

That the common centre of gravity of the earth, the sun, and all the planets is immovable.

For (by Cor. 4 of the Laws) that centre either is at rest or moves uniformly forward in a right line; but if that centre moved, the centre of the world would move also, against the Hypothesis.

PROPOSITION XII.   THEOREM XII.

That the sun is agitated by a perpetual motion, but never recedes far from the common centre of gravity of all the planets.

For since (by Cor. 2, Prop. VIII) the quantity of matter in the sun is to the quantity of matter in Jupiter as 1067 to 1; and the distance of Jupiter from the sun is to the semi-diameter of the sun in a proportion but a small matter greater, the common centre of gravity of Jupiter and the sun will fall upon a point a little without the surface of the sun. By the same argument, since the quantity of matter in the sun is to the quantity of matter in Saturn as 3021 to 1, and the distance of Saturn from the sun is to the semi-diameter of the sun in a proportion but a small matter less, the common centre of gravity of Saturn and the sun will fall upon a point a little within the surface of the sun. And, pursuing the principles of this computation, we should find that though the earth and all the planets were placed on one side of the sun, the distance of the common centre of gravity of all from the centre of the sun would scarcely amount to one diameter of the sun. In other cases, the distances of those centres are always less; and therefore, since that centre of gravity is in perpetual rest, the sun, according to the various positions of the planets, must perpetually be moved every way, but will never recede far from that centre.

Cor. Hence the common centre of gravity of the earth, the sun, and all the planets is to be esteemed the centre of the world; for since the earth, the sun, and all the planets mutually gravitate one towards another, and are therefore, according to their powers of gravity, in perpetual agitation, as the Laws of Motion require, it is plain that their movable centres cannot be taken for the immovable centre of the world. If that body were to be placed in the centre, towards which other bodies gravitate most (according to common opinion), that privilege ought to be allowed to the sun; but since the sun itself is moved, a fixed point is to be chosen from which the centre of the sun recedes least, and from which it would recede yet less if the body of the sun were denser and greater, and therefore less apt to be moved.

PROPOSITION XIII. THEOREM XIII.

The planets move in ellipses which have their common focus in the centre of the sun; and, by radii drawn to that centre, they describe areas proportional to the times of description.

We have discoursed above of these motions from the Phænomena. Now that we know the principles on which they depend, from those principles we deduce the motions of the heavens *a priori*. Because the weights of the planets towards the sun are reciprocally as the squares of their distances from the sun's centre, if the sun was at rest, and the other planets did not mutually act one upon another, their orbits would be ellipses, having the sun in their common focus; and they would describe areas proportional to the times *of description,* by Prop. I, Book One. But the mutual actions of the planets one upon another are so very small, that they may be neglected.

It is true that the action of Jupiter upon Saturn is not to be neglected: for the force of gravity towards Jupiter is to the force of gravity towards the sun as 1 to 1067; and therefore in the conjunction of Jupiter and Saturn, because the distance of Saturn from Jupiter is to the distance of Saturn from the sun almost as 4 to 9, the gravity of Saturn towards Jupiter will be to the gravity of Saturn towards the sun as 81 to 16×1067; or, as 1 to about 211. And hence arises a perturbation of the orb of Saturn in every conjunction of this planet with Jupiter, so sensible that astronomers are puzzled with it. As the planet is differently situated in these conjunctions, its eccentricity is sometimes augmented, sometimes diminished; its aphelion is sometimes carried forward, sometimes backward, and its mean motion is by turns accelerated and retarded; yet the whole error in its motion about the sun, though arising from so great a force, may be almost avoided (except in the mean motion) by placing the lower focus of its orbit in the common centre of gravity of Jupiter and the sun, and therefore that error, when it is greatest, scarcely exceeds two minutes; and the greatest error in the mean motion scarcely exceeds two minutes yearly. But in the conjunction of Jupiter and Saturn, the accelerative forces of gravity of the sun towards Saturn, of Jupiter towards Saturn, and of Jupiter towards the sun, are almost as 16, 81, and $\dfrac{16\times81\times3021}{25}$, or 156609; and therefore the difference of the forces of gravity of the sun towards Saturn, and of Jupiter towards Saturn, is to the force of gravity of Jupiter towards the sun as 65 to 156609, or as 1 to 2409. But the greatest power of Saturn to disturb the motion of Jupiter is proportional to this difference; and therefore the perturbation of the orbit of Jupiter is much less than that of Saturn's. The perturbations of the other orbits are yet far less, except that the orbit of the earth is sensibly disturbed by the moon. The common centre of gravity of the earth and moon moves in an ellipsis about the sun in the focus thereof, and, by a radius drawn to the sun, describes areas proportional to the times of description. But the earth in the meantime by a menstrual motion is revolved about this common centre.

PROPOSITION XIV. THEOREM XIV.

The aphelions and nodes of the orbits of the planets are fixed.

It is true that some inequalities may arise from the mutual actions of the planets and comets in their revolutions; but these will be so small that they may be here passed by.

Cor. 1. The fixed stars are immovable, seeing they keep the same position to the aphelions and nodes of the planets.

Cor. 2. And since these stars are liable to no sensible parallax from the annual motion of the earth, they can have no force, because of their immense distance, to produce any sensible effect in our system. Not to mention that the fixed stars, every where promiscuously dispersed in the heavens, by their contrary attractions destroy their mutual actions, by Prop. LXX, Book One.

SCHOLIUM

Since the planets near the sun (viz. Mercury, Venus, the Earth, and Mars) are so small that they can act with but little force upon each other, therefore their aphelions and nodes must be fixed, excepting in so far as they are disturbed by the actions of Jupiter and Saturn, and other higher bodies. And hence we may find, by the theory of gravity, that their aphelions move a little *in consequentia,* in respect of the fixed stars, and that in the sesquiplicate proportion of their several distances from the sun. So that if the aphelion of Mars, in the space of a hundred years, is carried 33′ 20″ *in consequentia,* in respect of the fixed stars, the aphelions of the Earth, of Venus, and of Mercury, will in a hundred years be carried forwards 17′ 40″, 10′ 53″, and 4′ 16″, respectively. But these motions are so inconsiderable that we have neglected them in this Proposition.

PROPOSITION XV. PROBLEM I.

To find the principal diameters of the orbits of the planets.

They are to be taken in the sub-sesquiplicate proportion of the periodic times.

PROPOSITION XVI. PROBLEM II.

To find the eccentricities and aphelions of the planets.

PROPOSITION XVII. THEOREM XV.

That the diurnal motions of the planets are uniform, and that the libration of the moon arises from its diurnal motion.

PROPOSITION XVIII. THEOREM XVI.

That the axes of the planets are less than the diameters drawn perpendicular to the axes.

The equal gravitation of the parts on all sides would give a spherical figure to the planets, if it was not for their diurnal revolution in a circle. By that circular motion it comes to pass that the parts receding from the axis endeavour to ascend about the equator; and therefore if the matter is in a fluid state, by its ascent towards the equator it will enlarge the diameters there, and by its descent towards the poles it will shorten the axis. So the diameter of Jupiter (by the concurring observations of astronomers) is found shorter betwixt pole and pole than from east to west. And, by the same argument, if our earth was not higher about the equator than at the poles, the seas would subside about the poles, and, rising towards the equator, would lay all things there under water.

PROPOSITION XIX. PROBLEM III.

To find the proportion of the axis of a planet to the diameters perpendicular thereto.

Our countryman, Mr. *Norwood,* measuring a distance of 995751 feet of *London* measure between *London* and *York,* in 1635, and observing the difference of latitudes to be 2° 28′, determined the measure of one degree to be 367196 feet of *London* measure, that is, 57300 *Paris* toises. M. *Picart,* measuring an arc of one degree, and 22′ 55″ of the meridian between *Amiens* and *Malvoisine,* found an arc of one degree to be 57060 *Paris* toises. M. *Cassini,* the father, measured the distance upon the meridian from the town of *Collioure* in *Roussillon* to the Observatory of *Paris;* and his son added the distance from the Observatory to the Citadel of *Dunkirk.* The whole distance was 486156½ toises and the difference of the latitudes of *Collioure* and *Dunkirk* was 8 degrees, and 31′ 11⅚″. Hence an arc of one degree appears to be 57061 *Paris* toises. And from these measures we conclude that the circumference of the earth is 123249600, and its semi-diameter 19615800 *Paris* feet, upon the supposition that the earth is of a spherical figure.

In the latitude of *Paris* a heavy body falling in a second of time describes 15 *Paris* feet, 1 inch, 1⅐ line, as above, that is, 2173 lines ⁷⁄₉. The weight of the body is diminished by the weight of the ambient air. Let us suppose the weight lost thereby to be $\frac{1}{11000}$ part of the whole weight; then that heavy body falling *in vacuo* will describe a height of 2174 lines in one second of time.

A body in every sidereal day of 23ʰ. 56′ 4″ uniformly revolving in a circle at the distance of 19615800 feet from the centre, in one second of time describes an arc of 1433,46 feet; the versed sine of which is 0,05236561 feet, or 7,54064 lines. And therefore the force with which bodies descend in the latitude of *Paris* is to the centrifugal force of bodies in the equator arising from the diurnal motion of the earth as 2174 to 7,54064.

The centrifugal force of bodies in the equator is to the centrifugal force with which bodies recede directly from the earth in the latitude of *Paris* 48° 50′ 10″ in the duplicate proportion of the radius to the cosine of the latitude, that is, as 7,54064 to 3,267. Add this force to the force with which bodies descend by their weight in the latitude of *Paris,* and a body, in the latitude of *Paris,* falling by its whole undiminished force of gravity, in the time of one second, will describe 2177,267 lines, or 15 *Paris* feet, 1 inch, and 5,267 lines. And the total force of gravity in that latitude will be to the centrifugal force of bodies in the equator of the earth as 2177,267 to 7,54064, or as 289 to 1.

Wherefore if APBQ represent the figure of the earth, now no longer spherical, but generated by the rotation of an ellipsis about its lesser axis PQ; and ACQ *qca* a canal full of water, reaching from the pole Q*q* to the centre C*c,* and thence rising to the equator A*a;* the weight of the water in the leg of the canal AC*ca* will be to the weight of water in the other leg QC*cq* as 289 to 288, because the centrifugal force arising from the circular motion sustains and takes off one of the 289 parts of the weight (in the one leg), and the weight of 288 in the other sustains the rest. But by computation I find that if the matter of the earth was all uniform, and without any motion, and its axis PQ were to the diameter AB as 100 to 101, the force of gravity in the place Q towards the earth would be to the force of gravity in the same place Q towards a sphere described about the

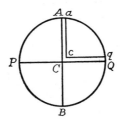

centre C with the radius PC, or QC, as 126 to 125. And, by the same argument, the force of gravity in the place A towards the spheroid generated by the rotation of the ellipsis APBQ about the axis AB is to the force of gravity in the same place A, towards the sphere described about the centre C with the radius AC, as 125 to 126. But the force of gravity in the place A towards the earth is a mean proportional betwixt the forces of gravity towards the spheroid and this sphere; because the sphere, by having its diameter PQ diminished in the proportion of 101 to 100, is transformed into the figure of the earth; and this figure, by having a third diameter perpendicular to the two diameters AB and PQ diminished in the same proportion, is converted into the said spheroid; and the force of gravity in A, in either case, is diminished nearly in the same proportion. Therefore the force of gravity in A towards the sphere described about the centre C with the radius AC is to the force of gravity in A towards the earth as 126 to 125½. And the force of gravity in the place Q towards the sphere described about the centre C with the radius QC, is to the force of gravity in the place A towards the sphere described about the centre C, with the radius AC, in the proportion of the diameters (by Prop. LXXII, Book One), that is, as 100 to 101. If, therefore, we compound those three proportions 126 to 125, 126 to 125½, and 100 to 101, into one, the force of gravity in the place Q towards the earth will be to the force of gravity in the place A towards the earth as 126×126×100 to 125×125½×101; or as 501 to 500.

Now since the force of gravity in either leg of the canal AC*ca,* or QC*cq,* is as the distance of the places from the centre of the earth, if those legs are conceived to be divided by transverse, parallel, and equidistant surfaces, into parts proportional to the wholes, the weights of any number of parts in the one leg AC*ca* will be to the weights of the same number of parts in the other leg as their magnitudes and the accelerative forces of their gravity conjunctly, that is, as 101 to 100, and 500 to 501, or as 505 to 501. And therefore if the centrifugal force of every part in the leg AC*ca,* arising from the diurnal motion, was to the weight of the same part as 4 to 505, so that from the weight of every part, conceived to be divided into 505 parts, the centrifugal force might take off four of those parts, the weights would remain equal in each leg, and therefore the fluid would rest in an equilibrium. But the centrifugal force of every part is to the weight of the same part as 1 to 289; that is, the centrifugal force, which should be $\frac{4}{505}$ parts of the weight, is only $\frac{1}{289}$ part thereof. And, therefore, I say, by the rule of proportion, that if the centrifugal force $\frac{4}{505}$ make the height of the water in the leg AC*ca* to exceed the height of the water in the leg QC*cq* by one $\frac{1}{100}$ part of its whole height, the centrifugal force $\frac{1}{289}$ will make the excess of the height in the leg AC*ca* only $\frac{1}{289}$ part of the height of the water in the other leg QC*cq;* and therefore the diameter of the earth at the equator, is to its diameter from pole to pole as 230 to 229. And since the mean semi-diameter of the earth, according to *Picart's* mensuration, is 19615800 *Paris* feet, or 3923,16 miles (reckoning 5000 feet to a mile), the earth will be higher at the equator than at the poles by 85472 feet, or $17\frac{1}{10}$ miles. And its height at the equator will be about 19658600 feet, and at the poles 19573000 feet.

If, the density and periodic time of the diurnal revolution remaining the same, the planet was greater or less than the earth, the proportion of the centrifugal force to that of gravity, and therefore also of the diameter betwixt the poles to the diameter at the equator, would likewise remain the same. But if the diurnal motion was accelerated or retarded in any proportion, the centrifugal force would be augmented or diminished nearly in the same duplicate proportion; and therefore the difference of the diameters will be increased or diminished in the same duplicate ratio very nearly. And if the density of the planet was augmented or diminished in any proportion, the force of gravity tending towards it would also be augmented or diminished in the same proportion: and the difference of the diameters contrariwise would be diminished in proportion as the force of gravity is augmented, and augmented in proportion as the force of gravity is diminished. Wherefore, since the earth, in respect of the fixed stars, revolves in 23^h. 56′, but Jupiter in 9^h. 56′, and the squares of their periodic times are as 29 to 5, and their densities as 400 to 94½, the difference of the diameters of Jupiter will be to its lesser diameter as $\frac{29}{5} \times \frac{400}{94\frac{1}{2}} \times \frac{1}{229}$ to 1, or as 1 to 9⅓, nearly. Therefore the diameter of Jupiter from east to west is to its diameter from pole to pole nearly as 10⅓ to 9⅓. Therefore since its greatest diameter is 37″, its lesser diameter lying between the poles will be 33″ 25‴. Add thereto about 3″ for the irregular refraction of light, and the apparent diameters of this planet will become 40″ and 36″ 25‴; which are to each other as 11⅛ to 10⅛, very nearly. These things are so upon the supposition that the body of Jupiter is uniformly dense. But now if its body be denser towards the plane of the equator than towards the poles, its diameters may be to each other as 12 to 11, or 13 to 12, or perhaps as 14 to 13.

And *Cassini* observed in the year 1691 that the diameter of Jupiter reaching from east to west is greater by about a fifteenth* part than the other diameter. Mr. *Pound* with his 123-feet telescope, and an excellent micrometer, measured the diameters of Jupiter in the year 1719 and found them as follow.

The Times.		Greatest diam.	Lesser diam.	The diam. to each other		
Day.	Hours.	Parts	Parts			
January 28	6	13,40	12,28	As 12	to	11
March 6	7	13,12	12,20	13¾	to	12¾
March 9	7	13,12	12,08	12⅔	to	11⅔
April 9	9	12,32	11,48	14½	to	13½

So that the theory agrees with the phænomena; for the planets are more heated by the sun's rays towards their equators, and therefore are a little more condensed by that heat than towards their poles.

Moreover, that there is a diminution of gravity occasioned by the diurnal rotation of the earth, and therefore the earth rises higher there than it does at the poles (supposing that its matter is uniformly dense), will appear by the experiments of pendulums related under the following Proposition.

PROPOSITION XX. PROBLEM IV.

To find and compare together the weights of bodies in the different regions of our earth.

Because the weights of the unequal legs of the canal of water ACQ-*qca* are equal; and the weights of the parts proportional to the whole legs, and alike situated in them, are one to another as the weights of the wholes, and therefore equal betwixt themselves; the weights of equal parts, and alike situated in the legs, will be reciprocally as the legs, that is, reciprocally as 230 to 229. And the case is the same in all homogeneous equal bodies alike situated in the legs of the canal. Their weights are reciprocally as the legs, that is, reciprocally as the distances of the bodies from the centre of the earth. Therefore if the bodies are situated in the uppermost parts of the canals, or on the surface of the earth, their weights will be one to another reciprocally as their distances from the centre. And, by the same argument, the weights in all other places round the whole surface of the earth are reciprocally as the distances of the places from the centre; and, therefore, in the hypothesis of the earth's being a spheroid are given in proportion.

Whence arises this Theorem, that the increase of weight in passing from the equator to the poles is nearly as the versed sine of double the latitude; or, which comes to the same thing, as the square of the right sine of the latitude; and the arcs of the degrees of latitude in the meridian

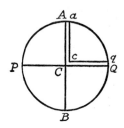

increase nearly in the same proportion. And, therefore, since the latitude of *Paris* is 48° 50', that of places under the equator 00° 00', and that of places under the poles 90°; and the versed sines of double those arcs are 11334,00000 and 20000, the radius being 10000; and the force of gravity at the pole is to the force of gravity at the equator as 230 to 229; and the excess of the force of gravity at the pole to the force of gravity at the equator as 1 to 229; the excess of the force of gravity in the latitude of *Paris* will be to the force of gravity at the equator as $1 \times {}^{11334}\!/_{20000}$ to 229, or as 5667 to 2290000. And therefore the whole forces of gravity in those places will be one to the other as 2295667 to 2290000. Wherefore since the lengths of pendulums vibrating in equal times are as the forces of gravity, and in the latitude of *Paris,* the length of a pendulum vibrating seconds is 3 *Paris* feet, and 8½ lines, or rather because of the weight of the air, 8⅝ lines, the length of a pendulum vibrating in the same time under the equator will be shorter by 1,087 lines. And by a like calculus the table on the following page is made.

By this table, therefore, it appears that the inequality of degrees is so small that the figure of the earth, in geographical matters, may be considered as spherical; especially if the earth be a little denser towards the plane of the equator than towards the poles.

Now several astronomers, sent into remote countries to make astronomical observations, have found that pendulum clocks do accordingly move slower near the equator than in our climates. And, first of all, in the year 1672 M. *Richer* took notice of it in the island of *Cayenne;* for when, in the month of *August,* he was observing the transits of the fixed stars over the meridian, he found his clock to go slower than it ought in respect of the mean motion of the sun at the rate of 2' 28" a day. Therefore, fitting up a simple pendulum to vibrate in seconds, which were measured by an excellent clock, he observed the length of that simple pendulum; and this he did over and over every week for ten months together. And upon his return to *France,* comparing the length of that pendulum with the length

Latitude of the place	Length of the pendulum		Measure of one degree in the meridian
Deg.	Feet	Lines.	Toises.
0	3 ·	7,468	56637
5	3 ·	7,482	56642
10	3 ·	7,526	56659
15	3 ·	7,596	56687
20	3 ·	7,692	56724
25	3 ·	7,812	56769
30	3 ·	7,948	56823
35	3 ·	8,099	56882
40	3 ·	8,261	56945
1	3 ·	8,294	56958
2	3 ·	8,327	56971
3	3 ·	8,361	56984
4	3 ·	8,394	56997
45	3 ·	8,428	57010
6	3 ·	8,461	57022
7	3 ·	8,494	57035
8	3 ·	8,528	57048
9	3 ·	8,561	57061
50	3 ·	8,594	57074
55	3 ·	8,756	57137
60	3 ·	8,907	57196
65	3 ·	9,044	57250
70	3 ·	9,162	57295
75	3 ·	9,258	57332
80	3 ·	9,329	57360
85	3 ·	9,372	57377
90	3 ·	9,387	57382

of the pendulum at *Paris* (which was 3 *Paris* feet and 8⅗ lines), he found it shorter by 1¼ line.

Afterwards, our friend Dr. *Halley,* about the year 1677, arriving at the island of St. *Helena,* found his pendulum clock to go slower there than at *London* without marking the difference. But he shortened the rod of his clock by more than the ⅛ of an inch, or 1½ line; and to effect this, because the length of the screw at the lower end of the rod was not sufficient, he interposed a wooden ring betwixt the nut and the ball.

Then, in the year 1682, M. *Varin* and M. *des Hayes* found the length of a simple pendulum vibrating in seconds at the Royal Observatory of *Paris* to be 3 feet and 8⅝ lines. And by the same method in the island of *Goree,* they found the length of an isochronal pendulum to be 3 feet and 6⅝ lines, differing from the former by two lines. And in the same year, going to the islands of *Guadaloupe* and *Martinico,* they found that the length of an isochronal pendulum in those islands was 3 feet and 6½ lines.

After this, M. *Couplet,* the son, in the month of *July* 1697, at the Royal Observatory of *Paris,* so fitted his pendulum clock to the mean motion of the sun that for a considerable time together the clock agreed with the motion of the sun. In *November* following, upon his arrival at *Lisbon,* he found his clock to go slower than before at the rate of 2′ 13″ in 24 hours. And next *March* coming to *Paraiba,* he found his clock to go slower than at *Paris,* and at the rate 4′ 12″ in 24 hours; and he affirms, that the pendulum vibrating in seconds was shorter at *Lisbon* by 2½ lines, and at *Paraiba* by 3⅔ lines, than at *Paris.* He had done better to have reckoned those differences 1⅓ and 2⅝: for these differences correspond to the differences of the times 2′ 13″ and 4′ 12″. But this gentleman's observations are so gross, that we cannot confide in them.

In the following years, 1699 and 1700, M. *des Hayes,* making another voyage to *America,* determined that in the island of *Cayenne* and *Granada* the length of the pendulum vibrating in seconds was a small matter less than 3 feet and 6½ lines; that in the island of St. *Christophers* it was 3 feet and 6¾ lines; and in the island of St. *Domingo* 3 feet and 7 lines.

And in the year 1704, P. *Feuillé,* at *Puerto Bello* in *America,* found that the length of the pendulum vibrating in seconds was 3 *Paris* feet, and only 5⁷⁄₁₂ lines, that is, almost 3 lines shorter than at *Paris;* but the observation was faulty. For afterward, going to the island of *Martinico,* he found the length of the isochronal pendulum there 3 *Paris* feet and 5¹⁰⁄₁₂ lines.

Now the latitude of *Paraiba* is 6° 38′ south; that of *Puerto Bello* 9° 33′ north; and the latitudes of the islands *Cayenne, Goree, Guadaloupe, Martinico, Granada,* St. *Christophers,* and St. *Domingo* are respectively 4° 55′, 14° 40″, 15° 00′, 14° 44′, 12° 06′, 17° 19′, and 19° 48′ north. And the excesses of the length of the pendulum at *Paris* above the lengths of the isochronal pendulums observed in those latitudes are a little greater than by the table of the lengths of the pendulum before computed. And therefore the earth is a little higher under the equator than by the preceding calculus, and a little denser at the centre than in mines near the surface, unless, perhaps, the heats of the torrid zone have a little extended the length of the pendulums.

For M. *Picart* has observed that a rod of iron, which in frosty weather in the winter season was one foot long, when heated by fire was lengthened into one foot and ¼ line. Afterward M. *de la Hire* found that a rod of iron, which in the like winter season was 6 feet long, when exposed to the heat of the summer sun, was extended into 6 feet and ⅔ line. In the former case the heat was greater than in the latter; but in the latter it was greater than the heat of the external parts of a human body; for metals exposed to the summer sun acquire a very considerable degree of heat. But the rod of a pendulum clock is never exposed to the heat of the summer sun, nor ever acquires a heat equal to that of the external parts of a human body; and, therefore, though the 3 feet rod of a pendulum clock will indeed be a little longer in the summer than in the winter season, yet the difference will scarcely amount to ¼ line. Therefore the total difference of the lengths of isochronal pendulums in different climates cannot be ascribed to the difference of heat; nor indeed to the mistakes of the *French* astronomers. For although there is not a perfect agreement betwixt their observations, yet the errors are so small that they may be neglected; and in this they all agree, that isochronal pendulums are shorter under the equator than at the Royal Observatory of *Paris,* by a difference not less than $1\frac{1}{4}$ line nor greater than $2\frac{2}{3}$ lines. By the observations of M. *Richer,* in the island of *Cayenne,* the difference was $1\frac{1}{4}$ line. That difference, being corrected by those of M. *des Hayes,* becomes $1\frac{1}{2}$ line or $1\frac{3}{4}$ line. By the less accurate observations of others, the same was made about two lines. And this disagreement might arise partly from the errors of the observations, partly from the dissimilitude of the internal parts of the earth, and the height of mountains; partly from the different heats of the air.

I take an iron rod of 3 feet long to be shorter by a sixth part of one line in winter time with us here in *England* than in the summer. Because of the great heats under the equator, subduct this quantity from the difference of one line and a quarter observed by M. *Richer,* and there will remain one line $\frac{1}{12}$, which agrees very well with $1\frac{87}{1000}$ line collected, by the theory a little before. M. *Richer* repeated his observations, made in the island of *Cayenne,* every week for ten months together, and compared the lengths of the pendulum which he had there noted in the iron rods with the lengths thereof which he observed in *France.* This diligence and care seems to have been wanting to the other observers. If this gentleman's observations are to be depended on, the earth is higher under the equator than at the poles, and that by an excess of about 17 miles; as appeared above by the theory.

PROPOSITION XXIV. THEOREM XIX.

That the flux and reflux of the sea arise from the actions of the sun and moon.

By Cor. 19 and 20, Prop. LXVI, Book One, it appears that the waters of the sea ought twice to rise and twice to fall every day, as well lunar as solar; and that the greatest height of the waters in the open and deep seas ought to follow the appulse of the luminaries to the meridian of the place by a less interval than 6 hours; as happens in all that eastern tract of the *Atlantic* and *Æthiopic* seas between *France* and the *Cape of Good Hope;* and on the coasts of *Chili* and *Peru* in the *South Sea;* in all which shores the flood falls out about the second, third, or fourth hour, unless where the motion propagated from the deep ocean is by the shallowness of the channels, through which it passes to some particular places, retarded to the fifth, sixth, or seventh hour, and even later. The hours I reckon from the appulse of each luminary to the meridian of the place, as well under as above the horizon; and by the hours of the lunar day I understand the 24th parts of that time which the moon, by its apparent diurnal motion, employs to come about again to the meridian of the place which it left the day before. The force of the sun or moon in raising the sea is greatest in the appulse of the luminary to the meridian of the place; but the force impressed upon the sea at that time continues a little while after the impression, and is afterwards increased by a new though less force still acting upon it. This makes the sea rise higher and higher, till this new force becoming too weak to raise it any more, the sea rises to its greatest height. And this will come to pass, perhaps, in one or two hours, but more frequently near the shores in about three hours, or even more, where the sea is shallow.

The two luminaries excite two motions, which will not appear distinctly, but between them will arise one mixed motion compounded out of both. In the conjunction or opposition of the luminaries their forces will be conjoined, and bring on the greatest flood and ebb. In the quadratures the sun will raise the waters which the moon depresses, and depress the waters which the moon raises, and from the difference of their forces the smallest of all tides will follow. And because (as experience tells us) the force of the moon is greater than that of the sun, the greatest height of the waters will happen about the third lunar hour. Out of the syzygies and quadratures, the greatest tide, which by the single force of the moon ought to fall out at the third lunar hour, and by the single force of the sun at the third solar hour, by the compounded forces of both must fall out in an intermediate time that approaches nearer to the third hour of the moon than to that of the sun. And, therefore, while the moon is passing from the syzygies to the quadratures, during which time the 3d hour of the sun precedes the 3d hour of the moon, the greatest height of the waters will also precede the 3d hour of the moon, and that, by the greatest interval, a little after the octants of the moon; and, by like intervals, the greatest tide will follow the 3d lunar hour, while the moon is passing from the quadratures to the syzygies. Thus it happens in the open sea; for in the mouths of rivers the greater tides come later to their height.

But the effects of the luminaries depend upon their distances from the earth; for when they are less distant, their effects are greater, and when more distant, their effects are less, and that in the triplicate proportion of their apparent diameter. Therefore it is that the sun, in the winter time, being then in its perigee, has a greater effect, and makes the tides in the syzygies something greater, and those in the quadratures something less than in the summer season; and every month the moon, while in the perigee, raises greater tides than at the distance of 15 days before or after, when it is in its apogee. Whence it comes to pass that two highest tides do not follow one the other in two immediately succeeding syzygies.

The effect of either luminary doth likewise depend upon its declination or distance from the equator; for if the luminary was placed at the pole, it would constantly attract all the parts of the waters without any intension or remission of its action, and could cause no reciprocation of motion. And, therefore, as the luminaries decline from the equator towards either pole, they will, by degrees, lose their force, and on this account will excite lesser tides in the solstitial than in the equinoctial syzygies. But in the solstitial quadratures they will raise greater tides than in the quadratures about the equinoxes; because the force of the moon, then situated in the equator, most exceeds the force of the sun. Therefore the greatest tides fall out in those syzygies, and the least in those quadratures, which happen about the time of both equinoxes: and the greatest tide in the syzygies is always succeeded by the least tide in the quadratures, as we find by experience. But, because the sun is less distant from the earth in winter than in summer, it comes to pass that the greatest and least tides more frequently appear before than after the vernal equinox, and more frequently after than before the autumnal.

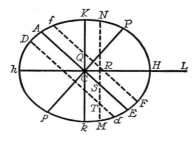

Moreover, the effects of the luminaries depend upon the latitudes of places. Let ApEP represent the earth covered with deep waters; C its centre; P, p its poles; AE the equator; F any place without the equator; Ff the parallel of the place; Dd the correspondent parallel on the other side of the equator; L the place of the moon three hours before; H the place of the earth directly under it; h the opposite place; K, k the places at 90 degrees distance; CH, Ch, the greatest heights of the sea from the centre of the earth; and CK, Ck, its least heights: and if with the axes Hh, Kk, an ellipsis is described, and by the revolution of that ellipsis about its longer axis Hh a spheroid HPKhpk is formed, this spheroid will nearly represent the figure of the sea; and CF, Cf, CD, Cd, will represent the heights of the sea in the places Ff, Dd. But farther; in the said revolution of the ellipsis any point N describes the circle NM cutting the parallels Ff, Dd, in any places RT, and the equator AE in S; CN will represent the height of the sea in all those places R, S, T, situated in this circle. Wherefore, in the diurnal revolution of any place F, the greatest flood will be in F, at the third hour after the appulse of the moon to the meridian above the horizon; and afterwards the greatest ebb in Q, at the third hour after the setting of the moon; and then the greatest flood in f, at the third hour after the appulse of the moon to the meridian under the horizon; and, lastly, the greatest ebb in Q, at the third hour after the rising of the moon; and the latter flood in f will be less than the preceding flood in F. For the whole sea is divided into two hemispherical floods, one in the hemisphere KHk on the north side, the other in the opposite hemisphere Khk, which we may therefore call the northern and the southern floods.

These floods, being always opposite the one to the other, come by turns to the meridians of all places, after an interval of 12 lunar hours. And seeing the northern countries partake more of the northern flood, and the southern countries more of the southern flood, thence arise tides, alternately greater and less in all places without the equator, in which the luminaries rise and set. But the greatest tide will happen when the moon declines towards the vertex of the place, about the third hour after the appulse of the moon to the meridian above the horizon; and when the moon changes its declination *to the other side of the equator,* that which was the greater tide will be changed into a lesser. And the greatest difference of the floods will fall out about the times of the solstices; especially if the ascending node of the moon is about the first of Aries. So it is found by experience that the morning tides in winter exceed those of the evening, and the evening tides in summer exceed those of the morning; at *Plymouth* by the height of one foot, but at *Bristol* by the height of 15 inches, according to the observations of *Colepress* and *Sturmy.*

But the motions which we have been describing suffer some alteration from that force of reciprocation, which the waters, being once moved, retain a little while *by their vis insita.* Whence it comes to pass that the tides may continue for some time, though the actions of the luminaries should cease. This power of retaining the impressed motion lessens the difference of the alternate tides, and makes those tides which immediately succeed after the syzygies greater, and those which follow next after the quadratures less. And hence it is that the alternate tides at *Plymouth* and *Bristol* do not differ much more one from the other than by the height of a foot or 15 inches, and that the greatest tides of all at those ports are not the first but the third after the syzygies. And, besides, all the motions are retarded in their passage through shallow channels, so that the greatest tides of all, in some straits and mouths of rivers, are the fourth or even the fifth after the syzygies.

Farther, it may happen that the tide may be propagated from the ocean through different channels towards the same port, and may pass quicker through some channels than through others; in which case the same tide, divided into two or more succeeding one another, may compound new motions of different kinds. Let us suppose two equal tides flowing towards the same port from different places, the one preceding the other by 6 hours; and suppose the first tide to happen at the third hour of the appulse of the moon to the meridian of the port. If the moon at the time of the appulse to the meridian was in the equator, every 6 hours alternately there would arise equal floods, which, meeting with as many equal ebbs, would so balance one the other that for that day the water would stagnate and remain quiet. If the moon then declined from the equator, the tides in the ocean would be alternately greater and less, as was said; and from thence two greater and two lesser tides would be alternately propagated towards that port. But the two greater floods would make the greatest height of the waters to fall out in the middle time betwixt both; and the greater and lesser floods would make the waters to rise to a mean height in the middle time between them, and in the middle time between the two lesser floods the waters would rise to their least height. Thus in the space of 24 hours the waters would come, not twice, as commonly, but once only to their greatest, and once only to their least height; and their greatest height, if the moon declined towards the elevated pole, would happen at the 6th or 30th hour after the appulse of the moon to the meridian; and when the moon changed its declination, this flood would be changed into an ebb. An example of all which Dr. *Halley* has given us, from the observations of seamen in the port of *Batsham,* in the kingdom of *Tunquin,* in the latitude of 20° 50′ north. In that port, on the day which follows after the passage of the moon over the equator, the waters stagnate: when the moon declines to the north, they begin to flow and ebb, not twice, as in other ports, but once only every day: and the flood happens at the setting, and the greatest ebb at the rising of the moon. This tide increases with the declination of the moon till the 7th or 8th day; then for the 7 or 8 days following it decreases at the same rate as it had increased before, and ceases when the moon changes its declination, crossing over the equator to the south. After which the flood is immediately changed into an ebb; and thenceforth the ebb happens at the setting and the flood at the rising of the moon; till the moon, again passing the equator, changes its declination. There are two inlets to this port and the neighboring channels, one from the seas of *China,* between the continent and the island of *Leuconia;* the other from the *Indian* sea, between the continent and the island of *Borneo.* But whether there be really two tides propagated through the said channels, one from the *Indian* sea in the space of 12 hours, and one from the sea of *China* in the space of 6 hours, which therefore happening at the 3d and 9th lunar hours, by being compounded together, produce those motions; or whether there be any other circumstances in the state of those seas, I leave to be determined by observations on the neighbouring shores.

Thus I have explained the causes of the motions of the moon and of the sea.

GENERAL SCHOLIUM

Bodies projected in our air suffer no resistance but from the air. Withdraw the air, as is done in Mr. *Boyle's* vacuum, and the resistance ceases; for in this void a bit of fine down and a piece of solid gold descend with equal velocity. And the parity of reason must take place in the celestial spaces above the earth's atmosphere; in which spaces, where there is no air to resist their motions, all bodies will move with the greatest freedom; and the planets and comets will constantly pursue their revolutions in orbits given in kind and position, according to the laws above explained; but though these bodies may, indeed, persevere in their orbits by the mere laws of gravity, yet they could by no means have at first derived the regular position of the orbits themselves from those laws.

The six primary planets are revolved about the sun in circles concentric with the sun, and with motions directed towards the same parts, and almost in the same plane. Ten moons are revolved about the earth, Jupiter and Saturn, in circles concentric with them, with the same direction of motion, and nearly in the planes of the orbits of those planets; but it is not to be conceived that mere mechanical causes could give birth to so many regular motions, since the comets range over all parts of the heavens in very eccentric orbits; for by that kind of motion they pass easily through the orbs of the planets, and with great rapidity; and in their aphelions, where they move the slowest, and are detained the longest, they recede to the greatest distances from each other, and thence suffer the least disturbance from their mutual attractions. This most beautiful system of the sun, planets, and comets could only proceed from the counsel and dominion of an intelligent and powerful Being. And if the fixed stars are the centres of other like systems, these, being formed by the like wise counsel, must be all subject to the dominion of One; especially since the light of the fixed stars is of the same nature with the light of the sun, and from every system light passes into all the other systems: and lest the systems of the fixed stars should, by their gravity, fall on each other mutually, he hath placed those systems at immense distances one from another.

Hitherto we have explained the phænomena of the heavens and of our sea by the power of gravity, but have not yet assigned the cause of this power. This is certain, that it must proceed from a cause that penetrates to the very centres of the sun and planets, without suffering the least diminution of its force; that operates not according to the quantity of the surfaces of the particles upon which it acts (as mechanical causes use to do), but according to the quantity of the solid matter which they contain, and propagates its virtue on all sides to immense distances, decreasing always in the duplicate proportion of the distances. Gravitation towards the sun is made up out of the gravitations towards the several particles of which the body of the sun is composed; and in receding from the sun decreases accurately in the duplicate proportion of the distances as far as the orb of Saturn, as evidently appears from the quiescence of the aphelions of the planets; nay, and even to the remotest aphelions of the comets, if those aphelions are also quiescent. But hitherto I have not been able to discover the cause of those properties of gravity from phænomena, and I frame no hypotheses; for whatever is not deduced from the phænomena is to be called an hypothesis; and hypotheses, whether metaphysical or physical, whether of occult qualities or mechanical, have no place in experimental philosophy. In this philosophy particular propositions are inferred from the phænomena, and afterwards rendered general by induction. Thus it was that the impenetrability, the mobility, and the impulsive force of bodies, and the laws of motion and of gravitation, were discovered. And to us it is enough that gravity does really exist, and act according to the laws which we have explained, and abundantly serves to account for all the motions of the celestial bodies, and of our sea.

And now we might add something concerning a certain most subtle

Spirit which pervades and lies hid in all gross bodies; by the force and action of which Spirit the particles of bodies mutually attract one another at near distances, and cohere, if contiguous; and electric bodies operate to greater distances, as well repelling as attracting the neighbouring corpuscles; and light is emitted, reflected, refracted, inflected, and heats bodies; and all sensation is excited, and the members of animal bodies move at the command of the will, namely, by the vibrations of this Spirit, mutually propagated along the solid filaments of the nerves, from the outward organs of sense to the brain, and from the brain into the muscles. But these are things that cannot be explained in few words, nor are we furnished with that sufficiency of experiments which is required to an accurate determination and demonstration of the laws by which this electric and elastic Spirit operates.

END OF THE MATHEMATICAL PRINCIPLES

RELATIVITY: THE SPECIAL AND GENERAL THEORY

by

ALBERT EINSTEIN

CONTENTS

Relativity: The Special and General Theory

ALBERT EINSTEIN

1879–1955

EINSTEIN's is undoubtedly the best known of modern scientists' names. His love of music and his skill as a violinist forgotten, his devotion to philanthropic causes and his services to international order neglected, he was still regarded as the type of scientist who lived in an intellectual atmosphere so rarefied that the layman dared not enter it. He is widely believed to have made science so abstruse and complicated that it retreated ever farther from the ambitious grasp. Yet he himself considered his object to be the increase of scientific clarity and simplicity.

Einstein was born in 1879 in Ulm, Württemberg, where his father owned a small electric-technical plant. In Munich he attended the Luitpold Gymnasium until 1894; then his family moved to Milan, and he entered the Cantonal School at Aarau, Switzerland. Two years later he began to attend lectures at the Technical Academy in Zurich, and shortly afterward, while still a student, he taught mathematics and physics in the same school. In 1901 he became a Swiss citizen, thus qualifying for a post as examiner of patents in Berne. He held this position for eight years. Meantime he married a fellow student, a Serbian girl; he served as an unsalaried lecturer in the University of Berne; and he began publishing his first important papers.

An early believer in Planck's quantum theory (1900), in these early papers Einstein treated problems which invited application of quantum mechanics. In one series (1905-09), on the assumption that propagated radiation has a "quantum-like" structure, he developed the light-quantum hypothesis, and a law of photoelectric effects. He made the first real extension of Planck's fundamental hypothesis in a paper (1907) on the variation of specific heat with temperature. Using the generalized Bohr atom rather than Planck's linear oscillator as his basic concept, he developed his Law of Radiation. Much earlier he had exhaustively studied the Brownian Movements —those erratic motions of microscopic particles of insoluble matter in still water. Though these movements observably demonstrated the kinetic theory of matter, they had puzzled physicists for eighty years. Now Einstein published a complete theory and working formulas to explain them.

Discussing the Brownian Movements when he was twenty-six, Einstein wrote that "rest and equilibrium can only be an outward semblance which marks a state of disorder and unrest and prepares us for a profound alteration in the aspect of the universe as soon as we alter the scale of our observations. . . . Nature is such that it is impossible to determine absolute motion by any experiment whatever." He was challenging the three-century-long reign of Newton's concept of the universe, signalizing the revolution in scientific thought which has transferred the study of the inner workings of nature from the engineering scientist to the mathematician.

The readers of these early papers recognized in them the scope of imagination and the boldness of deduction of a new master. In 1909 the University of Zurich, where shortly before he had earned his doctoral degree, made him professor extraordinary of theoretical physics; two years later he was named professor of physics at the University of Prague; the next year he returned to Zurich as professor of physics in the Technical Academy; and in 1913, after becoming once more a German citizen, he was named director of the Kaiser-Wilhelm Physical Institute in Berlin. He had now a stipend large enough to allow him to devote all his time, free of routine duties, to research; and he published constantly in the learned journals of Germany, Russia, Switzerland. The Academies of Copenhagen and of Amsterdam and the Royal Society elected him to membership. In 1921, for his work on the photochemical equivalent, the Nobel Prize was conferred upon him.

Six years prior to the award of the Nobel Prize, Einstein had published his generalized theory of relativity, and ten years before that, his restricted theory, with an account of its consequences. The restricted theory had been generally accepted in Germany as early as 1912; but elsewhere it was viewed skeptically. The complete theory made its way slowly, only gradually winning British scientists. By their vote Einstein was awarded the Copley Medal of the Royal Society in 1925, and the Davy Medal in the following year. Both awards were for the relativity theory.

Einstein's growing fame brought him urgent invitations to visit other countries. He had lectured in France in the early 1920s, eager to further friendliness between French and German scientists. Now he traveled to India, to China, Japan, Palestine—where he seconded Zionist ambition—to Latin America, England, the United States. Everywhere his vast learning, his modesty, his humanity, his intellectual honesty impressed his hearers. Universities everywhere conferred honorary degrees upon him, and learned societies everywhere pressed him for contributions to their journals. While he was on the Pacific Coast in 1932, Hitler came to power in Germany. When a "German physics" was promulgated, Einstein resigned his directorship of the Institute in Berlin. Almost immediately he became professor of mathematics in the Institute for Advanced Study of Princeton University. He became an American citizen in 1940 and lived in Princeton until his death in 1955.

Einstein's theory of relativity grew out of his supposition that the identity in our world of *inertial mass* as measured by Galileo and of *gravitational mass* as measured by Newton is not accidental. If it is not, the Newtonian physics does not explain as wide a range of physical phenomena as is desirable. Classical, or Galilean-Newtonian, physics had explained many natural phenomena in terms of simple forces acting along straight lines, had triumphantly developed astronomy, and, by assuming a mechanical "ether," had applied its principles to problems apparently not mechanical. But the Michelson-Morley experiment on the velocity of light propagation provided sound reasons for denying the existence of an "ether"; the planet Mercury did not behave quite according to the predictions of Newtonian astronomy; electro-magnetic phenomena could not be wholly explained in terms of simple forces. Einstein weighed these difficulties, restudied the fundamental assumptions of physical science, and produced the special theory of relativity.

The special theory makes it possible, by use of the Lorentz transformation, to translate the phenomena of any given inertial system into terms of any other similar system. But Einstein was able to imagine a system not inertial—in fact, to question whether an inertial system could really exist. In 1913, during a walking tour in the Engadine with a party which included Mme. Curie—one of the few mathematicians in Europe sufficiently skilled to discuss his ideas with him—he remarked to her, "What I need to know is what happens to the passengers in an elevator when it falls into emptiness." This problem is not susceptible to experimental solution. But Einstein was a mathematician, not an experimentalist. He did solve the problem, and the answer is the general theory of relativity.

This theory requires that energy and mass being interchangeable and similar in properties, energy—in the form of light, for example—must have weight. It will, therefore, be deflected in a strong gravitational field. During the eclipse of the sun in 1919, observation startlingly confirmed the theory. Light from the fixed stars was deflected in the neighborhood of the sun, and exactly in the direction and to the amount which Einstein had computed. The theory also satisfactorily explained the aberration in the path of Mercury; using the Maxwell equations, it accounted for the phenomena of electromagnetism. Further, it foretold atomic fission and the transmutation of one element into another, ideas which later skilled experimentation confirmed.

These triumphant demonstrations have led to general acceptance of the theory of relativity, and thus to modern physics. But modern physics differs radically from Newtonian physics. Indeed, it provides a wholly new concept of the physical universe—one in which a mechanical ether does not exist, in which mass and energy are interchangeable, in which absolute rest is impossible, and in which absolute time is unrecognized. Properly the twentieth century may claim to add to the list of builders of world concepts—Pythagoras, Copernicus, Newton—one more: Einstein.

What follows is a condensation of Einstein's *Relativity: The Special and General Theory,* written while he was professor of physics in the University of Berlin.

RELATIVITY

PART ONE: THE SPECIAL THEORY OF RELATIVITY

I. PHYSICAL MEANING OF GEOMETRICAL PROPOSITIONS

GEOMETRY sets out from certain conceptions such as "plane," "point," and "straight line," with which we are able to associate more or less definite ideas, and from certain simple propositions (axioms) which, in virtue of these ideas, we are inclined to accept as "true." Then, on the basis of a logical process, the justification of which we feel ourselves compelled to admit, all remaining propositions are shown to follow from those axioms, *i.e.* they are proven.

If, in pursuance of our habit of thought, we now supplement the propositions of Euclidean geometry by the single proposition that two points on a practically rigid body always correspond to the same distance (line-interval), independently of any changes in position to which we may subject the body, the propositions of Euclidean geometry then resolve themselves into propositions on the possible relative position of practically rigid bodies. Geometry which has been supplemented in this way is then to be treated as a branch of physics. We can now legitimately ask as to the "truth" of geometrical propositions interpreted in this way.

II. THE SYSTEM OF CO-ORDINATES

EVERY DESCRIPTION of the scene of an event or of the position of an object in space is based on the specification of the point on a rigid body (body of reference) with which that event or object coincides. This applies not only to scientific description, but also to everyday life. If I analyse the place specification "Trafalgar Square, London," I arrive at the following result. The earth is the rigid body to which the specification of place refers; "Trafalgar Square, London" is a well-defined point, to which a name has been assigned, and with which the event coincides in space. If a cloud is hovering over Trafalgar Square, then we can determine its position relative to the surface of the earth by erecting a pole perpendicularly on the Square, so that it reaches the cloud. The length of the pole measured with the standard measuring rod, combined with the specification of the position of the foot of the pole, supplies us with a complete place specification.

(*a*) We imagine the rigid body, to which the place specification is referred, supplemented in such a manner that the object whose position we require is reached by the completed rigid body.

(*b*) In locating the position of the object, we make use of a number (here the length of the pole measured with the measuring rod) instead of designated points of reference.

(*c*) We speak of the height of the cloud even when the pole which reaches the cloud has not been erected. By means of optical observations of the cloud from different positions on the ground, and taking into account the properties of the propagation of light, we determine the length of the pole we should have required in order to reach the cloud.

From this consideration we see that it will be advantageous if, in the description of position, it should be possible by means of numerical measures to make ourselves independent of the existence of marked positions (possessing names) on the rigid body of reference. In the physics of measurement this is attained by the application of the Cartesian system of co-ordinates.

This consists of three plane surfaces perpendicular to each other and rigidly attached to a rigid body. Referred to a system of co-ordinates, the scene of any event will be determined (for the main part) by the specification of the lengths of the three perpendiculars or co-ordinates (x, y, z) which can be dropped from the scene of the event to those three plane surfaces.

We thus obtain the following result: Every description of events in space involves the use of a rigid body to which such events have to be referred. The resulting relationship takes for granted that the laws of Euclidean geometry hold for "distances," the "distance" being represented physically by means of the convention of two marks on a rigid body.

III. SPACE AND TIME IN CLASSICAL MECHANICS

"The purpose of mechanics is to describe how bodies change their position in space with time."

It is not clear what is to be understood here by "position" and "space." I stand at the window of a railway carriage which is travelling uniformly, and drop a stone on the embankment, without throwing it. Then, disregarding the influence of the air resistance, I see the stone descend in a straight line. A pedestrian who observes the misdeed from the footpath notices that the stone falls to earth in a parabolic curve. I now ask: Do the "positions" traversed by the stone lie "in reality" on a straight line or on a parabola? Moreover, what is meant here by motion "in space"? From the considerations of the previous chapter the answer is self-evident. In the first place, we entirely shun the vague word "space," of which, we must honestly acknowledge, we cannot form the slightest conception, and we replace it by "motion relative to a practically rigid body of reference." If instead of "body of reference" we insert "system of co-ordinates," which is a useful idea for mathematical description, we are in a position to say: The stone traverses a straight line relative to a system of co-ordinates rigidly attached to the carriage, but relative to a system of co-ordinates rigidly attached to the ground (embankment) it describes a parabola. With the aid of this example it is clearly seen that there is no such thing as an independently existing trajectory (lit. "path-curve"), but only a trajectory relative to a particular body of reference.

In order to have a *complete* description of the motion, we must specify how the body alters its position *with time; i.e.* for every point on the trajectory it must be stated at what time the body is situated there. These data must be supplemented by such a definition of time that, in virtue of this definition, these time-values can be regarded essentially as magnitudes (results of measurements) capable of observation. If we take our stand on the ground of classical mechanics, we can satisfy this requirement for our illustration in the following manner. We imagine two clocks of identical construction; the man at the railway-carriage window is holding one of them, and the man on the footpath the other. Each of the observers determines the position on his own reference-body occupied by the stone at each tick of the clock he is holding in his hand. In this connection we have not taken account of the inaccuracy involved by the finiteness of the velocity of propagation of light.

IV. THE GALILEIAN SYSTEM OF CO-ORDINATES

As is well known, the fundamental law of the mechanics of Galilei-Newton, which is known as the *law of inertia,* can be stated thus: A body removed sufficiently far from other bodies continues in a state of rest or of uniform motion in a straight line. This law not only says something about the motion of the bodies, but it also indicates the reference-bodies or systems of co-ordinates, permissible in mechanics, which can be used in mechanical description. The visible fixed stars are bodies for which the law of inertia certainly holds to a high degree of approximation. Now if we use a system of co-ordinates which is rigidly attached to the earth, then, relative to this sytem, every fixed star describes a circle of immense radius in the course of an astronomical day, a result which is opposed to the statement of the law of inertia. So that if we adhere to this law we must refer these motions only to systems of co-ordinates relative to which the fixed stars do not move in a circle. A system of co-ordinates of which the state of motion is such that the law of inertia holds relative to it is called a "Galileian system of co-ordinates." The laws of the mechanics of Galilei-Newton can be regarded as valid only for a Galileian system of co-ordinates.

V. THE PRINCIPLE OF RELATIVITY (IN THE RESTRICTED SENSE)

IN ORDER TO ATTAIN the greatest possible clearness, let us return to our example of the railway carriage supposed to be travelling uniformly. We call its motion a uniform translation ("uniform" because it is of constant velocity and direction, "translation" because although the carriage changes its position relative to the embankment yet it does not rotate in so doing). Let us imagine a raven flying through the air in such a manner that its motion, as observed from the embankment, is uniform and in a straight line. If we were to observe the flying raven from the moving railway carriage, we should find that the motion of the raven would be one of different velocity and direction, but that it would still be uniform and in a straight line. Expressed in an abstract manner, we may say: If a mass m is moving uniformly in a straight line with respect to a co-ordinate system K, then it will also be moving uniformly and in a straight line relative to a second co-ordinate system K', provided that the latter is executing a uniform translatory motion with respect to K. In accordance with the discussion contained in the preceding section, it follows that: If, relative to K, K' is a uniformly moving co-ordinate system devoid of rotation, then natural phenomena run their course with respect to K' according to exactly the same general laws as with respect to K. This statement is called the *principle of relativity* (in the restricted sense).

As long as one was convinced that all natural phenomena were capable of representation with the help of classical mechanics, there was no need to doubt the validity of this principle of relativity. But in view of the more recent development of electrodynamics and optics it became more and more evident that classical mechanics affords an insufficient foundation for the physical description of all natural phenomena. At this juncture the question of the validity of the principle of relativity became ripe for discussion.

There are two general facts which at the outset speak very much in favour of the validity of the principle of relativity. It supplies us with the actual motions of the heavenly bodies with a delicacy of detail little short of wonderful. The principle of relativity must therefore apply with great accuracy in the domain of *mechanics*. But that a principle of such broad generality should hold with such exactness in one domain of phenomena, and yet should be invalid for another, is *a priori* not very probable.

We now proceed to the second argument. If the principle of relativity (in the restricted sense) does not hold, we should be constrained to believe that natural laws are capable of being formulated in a particularly simple manner, and of course only on condition that, from amongst all possible Galileian co-ordinate systems, we should have chosen *one* (K_0) of a particular state of motion as our body of reference. We should then be justified in calling this system "absolutely at rest," and all other Galileian systems K "in motion." If, for instance, our embankment were the system K_0, then our railway carriage would be a system K, relative to which less simple laws would hold than with respect to K_0. This diminished simplicity would be due to the fact that the carriage K would be in motion (*i.e.* "really") with respect to K_0. In the general laws of nature which have been formulated with reference to K, the magnitude and direction of the velocity of the carriage would necessarily play a part. Now in virtue of its motion in an orbit round the sun, our earth is comparable with a railway carriage travelling with a velocity of about 30 kilometres per second. If the principle of relativity were not valid we should therefore expect that the direction of motion of the earth at any moment would enter into the laws of nature, and also that physical systems in their behaviour would be dependent on the orientation in space with respect to the earth. For owing to the alteration in direction of the velocity of revolution of the earth in the course of a year, the earth cannot be at rest relative to the hypothetical system K_0 throughout the whole year. However, the most careful observations have never revealed such anisotropic properties in terrestrial physical space, *i.e.* a physical non-equivalence of different directions. This is a very powerful argument in favour of the principle of relativity.

VI. THE THEOREM OF THE ADDITION OF VELOCITIES EMPLOYED IN CLASSICAL MECHANICS

LET US SUPPOSE our old friend the railway carriage to be travelling along the rails with a constant velocity v, and that a man traverses the length of the carriage in the direction of travel with a velocity w. With what velocity W does the man advance relative to the embankment during the process? If the man were to stand still for a second, he would advance relative to the embankment through a distance v equal numerically to the velocity of the carriage. As a consequence of his walking, however, he traverses an additional distance w relative to the carriage, and hence also relative to the embankment, in this second, the distance w being numerically equal to the velocity with which he is walking. Thus in total he covers the distance $W = v + w$ relative to the embankment in the second considered.

VII. THE APPARENT INCOMPATIBILITY OF THE LAW OF PROPAGATION OF LIGHT WITH THE PRINCIPLE OF RELATIVITY

THERE IS HARDLY a simpler law in physics than that according to which light is propagated in empty space. Every child at school knows, or believes he knows, that this propagation takes place in straight lines with a velocity $c = 300,000$ km./sec.

Of course we must refer the process of the propagation of light (and indeed every other process) to a rigid reference-body (co-ordinate system).

As such a system let us again choose our embankment. We shall imagine the air above it to have been removed. If a ray of light be sent along the embankment, we see from the above that the tip of the ray will be transmitted with the velocity c relative to the embankment. Now let us suppose that our railway carriage is again travelling along the railway lines with the velocity v, and that its direction is the same as that of the ray of light, but its velocity of course much less. It is obvious that we can here apply the consideration of the previous section, since the ray of light plays the part of the man walking along relatively to the carriage. w is the required velocity of light with respect to the carriage, and we have

$$w = c - v.$$

The velocity of propagation of a ray of light relative to the carriage thus comes out smaller than c.

But this result comes into conflict with the principle of relativity set forth in Chapter V. For, like every other general law of nature, the law of the transmission of light *in vacuo* must, according to the principle of relativity, be the same for the railway carriage as reference-body as when the rails are the body of reference. But if every ray of light is propagated relative to the embankment with the velocity c, then for this reason it would appear that another law of propagation of light must necessarily hold with respect to the carriage—a result contradictory to the principle of relativity.

In view of this dilemma there appears to be nothing else for it than to abandon either the principle of relativity or the simple law of the propagation of light *in vacuo*. The epoch-making theoretical investigations of H. A. Lorentz on the electrodynamical and optical phenomena connected with moving bodies lead conclusively to a theory of electromagnetic phenomena, of which the law of the constancy of the velocity of light *in vacuo* is a necessary consequence. Prominent theoretical physicists were therefore more inclined to reject the principle of relativity.

At this juncture the theory of relativity entered the arena. As a result of an analysis of the physical conceptions of time and space, it became evident that *in reality there is not the least incompatibility between the principle of relativity and the law of propagation of light,* and that by systematically holding fast to both these laws a logically rigid theory could be arrived at. This theory has been called the *special theory of relativity.*

VIII. ON THE IDEA OF TIME IN PHYSICS

Lightning has struck the rails on our railway embankment at two places A and B far distant from each other. I make the additional assertion that these two lightning flashes occurred simultaneously. If I now approach you with the request to explain to me the sense of the statement more precisely, you find after some consideration that the answer to this question is not so easy as it appears at first sight.

After thinking the matter over for some time you offer the following suggestion with which to test simultaneity. By measuring along the rails, the connecting line AB should be measured and an observer placed at the mid-point M of the distance AB. This observer should be supplied with an arrangement (*e.g.* two mirrors inclined at 90°) which allows him visually to observe both places A and B at the same time. If the observer perceives the two flashes of lightning at the same time, then they are simultaneous.

I am very pleased with this suggestion. You declare: "There is only *one* demand to be made of the definition of simultaneity, namely, that in every real case it must supply us with an empirical decision as to whether or not the conception that has to be defined is fulfilled. That light requires the same time to traverse the path $A\longrightarrow M$ as for the path $B\longrightarrow M$ is in reality neither a *supposition nor a hypothesis* about the physical nature of light, but a *stipulation*."

It is clear that this definition can be used to give an exact meaning not only to *two* events, but to as many events as we care to choose, and independently of the positions of the scenes of the events with respect to the body of reference (here the railway embankment). We are thus led also to a definition of "time" in physics. For this purpose we suppose that clocks of identical construction are placed at the points A, B and C of the railway line (co-ordinate system), and that they are set in such a manner that the positions of their pointers are simultaneously (in the above sense) the same. Under these conditions we understand by the "time" of an event the reading (position of the hands) of that one of these clocks which is in the immediate vicinity (in space) of the event. In this manner a time-value is associated with every event which is essentially capable of observation.

IX. THE RELATIVITY OF SIMULTANEITY

We suppose a very long train travelling along the rails with the constant velocity v and in the direction indicated in Fig. 1. People travelling in this train will with advantage use the train as a rigid reference-body (co-

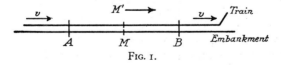

Fig. 1.

ordinate system); they regard all events in reference to the train. Then every event which takes place along the line also takes place at a particular point of the train.

Are two events (*e.g.* the two strokes of lightning A and B) which are simultaneous *with reference to the railway embankment* also simultaneous *relatively to the train?*

When we say that the lightning strokes A and B are simultaneous with respect to the embankment, we mean: the rays of light emitted at the places A and B, where the lightning occurs, meet each other at the mid-point M of the length A——$\rightarrow$$B$ of the embankment. But the events A and B also correspond to positions A and B on the train. Let M' be the mid-point of the distance A——$\rightarrow$$B$ on the travelling train. Just when the flashes of lightning occur, this point M' naturally coincides with the point M, but it moves towards the right in the diagram with the velocity v of the train. If an observer sitting in the position M' in the train did not possess this velocity, then he would remain permanently at M, and the light rays emitted by the flashes of lightning A and B would reach him simultaneously, *i.e.* they would meet just where he is situated. Now in reality (considered with reference to the railway embankment) he is hastening towards the beam of light coming from B, whilst he is riding on ahead of the beam of light coming from A. Hence the observer will see the beam of light emitted from B earlier than he will see that emitted from A. Observers who take the railway train as their reference-body must therefore come to the conclusion that the lightning flash B took place earlier than the lightning flash A. We thus arrive at the important result:

Events which are simultaneous with reference to the embankment are not simultaneous with respect to the train, and *vice versa* (relativity of simultaneity). Every reference-body (co-ordinate system) has its own particular time; unless we are told the reference-body to which the statement of time refers, there is no meaning in a statement of the time of an event.

We concluded that the man in the carriage, who traverses the distance w *per second* relative to the carriage, traverses the same distance also with respect to the embankment *in each second* of time. But, according to the foregoing considerations, the time required by a particular occurrence with respect to the carriage must not be considered equal to the duration of the same occurrence as judged from the embankment (as reference-body). Hence it cannot be contended that the man in walking travels the distance w relative to the railway line in a time which is equal to one second as judged from the embankment.

X. ON THE RELATIVITY OF THE CONCEPTION OF DISTANCE

LET US CONSIDER two particular points on the train travelling along the embankment with the velocity v, and inquire as to their distance apart. It is the simplest plan to use the train itself as the reference-body (co-ordinate system). An observer in the train measures the interval by marking off his measuring rod in a straight line (*e.g.* along the floor of the carriage) as many times as is necessary to take him from the one marked point to the other.

It is a different matter when the distance has to be judged from the railway line. If we call A' and B' the two points on the train whose distance apart is required, then both of these points are moving with the velocity v along the embankment. In the first place we require to determine the points A and B of the embankment which are just being passed by the two points A' and B' at a particular time t—judged from the embankment. These points A and B of the embankment can be determined by applying the definition of time given in Chapter VIII. The distance between these points A and B is then measured by repeated application of the measuring rod along the embankment.

A priori it is by no means certain that this last measurement will supply us with the same result as the first. Thus the length of the train as measured from the embankment may be different from that obtained by measuring in the train itself. This circumstance leads us to a second objection which must be raised against the apparently obvious consideration of Chapter VI. Namely, if the man in the carriage covers the distance w in a unit of time—*measured from the train*—then this distance—*as measured from the embankment*—is not necessarily also equal to w.

XI. THE LORENTZ TRANSFORMATION

THE RESULTS of the last three chapters show that the apparent incompatibility of the law of propagation of light with the principle of relativity (Chapter VII) has been derived by means of a consideration which borrowed two unjustifiable hypotheses from classical mechanics; these are as follows:

(1) The time-interval (time) between two events is independent of the condition of motion of the body of reference.
(2) The space-interval (distance) between two points of a rigid body is independent of the condition of motion of the body of reference.

If we drop these hypotheses, then the dilemma of Chapter VII disappears, because the theorem of the addition of velocities derived in Chapter VI becomes invalid. The possibility presents itself that the law of the propagation of light *in vacuo* may be compatible with the principle of relativity. In the discussion of Chapter VI we have to do with places and times relative both to the train and to the embankment. Can we conceive of a relation between place and time of the individual events relative to both reference-bodies, such that every ray of light possesses the velocity of transmission c relative to the embankment and relative to the train?

Up to the present we have only considered events taking place along the embankment, which had mathematically to assume the function of a straight line. In the manner indicated in Chapter II we can imagine this reference-body supplemented laterally and in a vertical direction by means of a framework of rods, so that an event which takes place anywhere can be localised with reference to this framework. Similarly, we can imagine the train travelling with the velocity v to be continued across the whole of space, so that every event, no matter how far off it may be, could also be localised with respect to the second framework. In every such framework we imagine three surfaces perpendicular to each other marked out, and designated as "co-ordinate planes" ("co-ordinate system"). A co-ordinate system K then corresponds to the embankment, and a co-ordinate system K' to the train. An event, wherever it may have taken place, would be fixed in space with respect to K by the three perpendiculars x, y, z on the co-ordinate planes, and with regard to time by a time-value t. Relative to K', *the same event* would be fixed in respect of space and time by corresponding values x', y', z', t', which of course are not identical with x, y, z, t.

What are the values x', y', z', t' of an event with respect to K', when the magnitudes x, y, z, t of the same event with respect to K are given? The relations must be so chosen that the law of the transmission of light

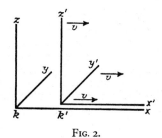

Fig. 2.

in vacuo is satisfied for one and the same ray of light (and of course for every ray) with respect to K and K'. For the relative orientation in space of the co-ordinate systems indicated in the diagram (Fig. 2), this problem is solved by means of the equations:

$$x' = \frac{x - vt}{\sqrt{1 - \dfrac{v^2}{c^2}}}$$

$$y' = y$$
$$z' = z$$

$$t' = \frac{t - \dfrac{v}{c^2} \cdot x}{\sqrt{1 - \dfrac{v^2}{c^2}}}$$

This system of equations is known as the "Lorentz transformation."

If in place of the law of transmission of light we had taken as our basis the tacit assumptions of the older mechanics as to the absolute character of times and lengths, then instead of the above we should have obtained the following equations:

$$x' = x - vt$$
$$y' = y$$
$$z' = z$$
$$t' = t.$$

This system of equations is often termed the "Galilei transformation." The Galilei transformation can be obtained from the Lorentz transformation by substituting an infinitely large value for the velocity of light c in the latter transformation.

XII. THE BEHAVIOUR OF MEASURING RODS AND CLOCKS IN MOTION

I PLACE a metre-rod in the x'-axis of K' in such a manner that one end (the beginning) coincides with the point $x' = 0$, whilst the other end (the end of the rod) coincides with the point $x' = 1$. What is the length of the metre-rod relatively to the system K? In order to learn this, we need only ask where the beginning of the rod and the end of the rod lie with respect to K at a particular time t of the system K. By means of the first equation of the Lorentz transformation the values of these two points at the time $t = 0$ can be shown to be

$$x(\text{beginning of rod}) = 0 . \sqrt{1 - \frac{v^2}{c^2}}$$

$$x(\text{end of rod}) = 1 . \sqrt{1 - \frac{v^2}{c^2}},$$

the distance between the points being $\sqrt{1 - \frac{v^2}{c^2}}$. But the metre-rod

is moving with the velocity v relative to K. It therefore follows that the length of a rigid metre-rod moving in the direction of its length with a velocity v is $\sqrt{1 - v^2/c^2}$ of a metre. The rigid rod is thus shorter when in motion than when at rest, and the more quickly it is moving, the shorter is the rod. For the velocity $v = c$ we should have $\sqrt{1 - v^2/c^2} = 0$, and for still greater velocities the square root becomes imaginary. From this we conclude that in the theory of relativity the velocity c plays the part of a limiting velocity, which can neither be reached nor exceeded by any real body.

If, on the contrary, we had considered a metre-rod at rest in the x-axis with respect to K, then we should have found that the length of the rod as judged from K' would have been $\sqrt{1 - v^2/c^2}$; this is quite in accordance with the principle of relativity which forms the basis of our considerations. If we had based our considerations on the Galilei transformation we should not have obtained a contraction of the rod as a consequence of its motion.

Let us now consider a seconds clock which is permanently situated at the origin ($x' = 0$) of K'; $t' = 0$ and $t' = 1$ are two successive ticks of this clock. The first and fourth equations of the Lorentz transformation give for these two ticks:

$$t = 0$$

and

$$t = \frac{1}{\sqrt{1 - \frac{v^2}{c^2}}}.$$

As judged from K, the clock is moving with the velocity v; as judged from this reference-body, the time which elapses between two strokes of the clock is not one second, but $\dfrac{1}{\sqrt{1 - \dfrac{v^2}{c^2}}}$ seconds, *i. e.* a somewhat

larger time. As a consequence of its motion the clock goes more slowly than when at rest. Here also the velocity c plays the part of an unattainable limiting velocity.

XIII.   THEOREM OF THE ADDITION OF VELOCITIES. THE EXPERIMENT OF FIZEAU

In Chapter VI we derived the theorem of the addition of velocities in one direction in the form which also results from the hypotheses of classical mechanics. This theorem can also be deduced readily from the Galilei transformation (Chapter XI). In place of the man walking inside the carriage, we introduce a point moving relatively to the co-ordinate system K' in accordance with the equation

$$x' = wt'.$$

By means of the first and fourth equations of the Galilei transformation we can express x' and t' in terms of x and t, and we then obtain

$$x = (v + w)t.$$

This equation expresses nothing else than the law of motion of the point with reference to the system K (of the man with reference to the embankment). We denote this velocity by the symbol W, and we then obtain, as in Chapter VI,

$$W = v + w \dotfill \text{(A).}$$

But we can carry out this consideration just as well on the basis of the theory of relativity. In the equation

$$x' = wt'$$

we must then express x' and t' in terms of x and t, making use of the first and fourth equations of the *Lorentz transformation*. Instead of the equation (A) we then obtain the equation

$$W = \frac{v + w}{1 + \dfrac{vw}{c^2}} \quad \dots\dots\dots\dots\dots\dots\dots (B),$$

which corresponds to the theorem of addition for velocities in one direction according to the theory of relativity. The question now arises as to which of these two theorems is the better in accord with experience. On this point we are enlightened by a most important experiment which the brilliant physicist Fizeau performed more than half a century ago.

The experiment is concerned with the following question. Light travels in a motionless liquid with a particular velocity w. How quickly does it travel in the direction of the arrow in the tube T (see the accompanying diagram, Fig. 3) when the liquid above mentioned is flowing through the tube with a velocity v?

In accordance with the principle of relativity we shall certainly have to take for granted that the propagation of light always takes place with the same velocity w *with respect to the liquid,* whether the latter is in motion with reference to other bodies or not. The velocity of light relative to the liquid and the velocity of the latter relative to the tube are thus known, and we require the velocity of light relative to the tube.

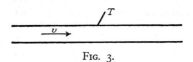

Fig. 3.

If we denote the velocity of the light relative to the tube by W, then this is given by the equation (A) or (B), according as the Galilei transformation or the Lorentz transformation corresponds to the facts. Experiment decides in favour of equation (B) derived from the theory of relativity, and the agreement is, indeed, very exact.

XIV. THE HEURISTIC VALUE OF THE THEORY OF RELATIVITY

OUR TRAIN OF THOUGHT in the foregoing pages can be epitomised in the following manner.

Every general law of nature must be so constituted that it is transformed into a law of exactly the same form when, instead of the space-time variables x, y, z, t of the original co-ordinate system K, we introduce new space-time variables x', y', z', t' of a co-ordinate system K'. In this connection the relation between the ordinary and the accented magnitudes is given by the Lorentz transformation. Or, in brief: General laws of nature are co-variant with respect to Lorentz transformations.

This is a definite mathematical condition that the theory of relativity demands of a natural law, and in virtue of this, the theory becomes a valuable heuristic aid in the search for general laws of nature. If a general law of nature were to be found which did not satisfy this condition, then at least one of the two fundamental assumptions of the theory would have been disproved. Let us now examine what general results the latter theory has hitherto evinced.

XV.   GENERAL RESULTS OF THE THEORY

It is clear from our previous considerations that the (special) theory of relativity has grown out of electrodynamics and optics. In these fields it has not appreciably altered the predictions of theory, but it has considerably simplified the theoretical structure, *i.e.* the derivation of laws, and—what is incomparably more important—it has considerably reduced the number of independent hypotheses forming the basis of theory.

Classical mechanics required to be modified before it could come into line with the demands of the special theory of relativity. For the main part, however, this modification affects only the laws for rapid motions, in which the velocities of matter v are not very small as compared with the velocity of light. We have experience of such rapid motions only in the case of electrons and ions; for other motions the variations from the laws of classical mechanics are too small to make themselves evident in practice. In accordance with the theory of relativity the kinetic energy of a material point of mass m is no longer given by the well-known expression

$$m \frac{v^2}{2},$$

but by the expression

$$\frac{mc^2}{\sqrt{1 - \frac{v^2}{c^2}}}.$$

This expression approaches infinity as the velocity v approaches the velocity of light c. The velocity must therefore always remain less than c, however great may be the energies used to produce the acceleration. If we develop the expression for the kinetic energy in the form of a series, we obtain

$$mc^2 + m\,\frac{v^2}{2} + \frac{3}{8}\,m\,\frac{v^4}{c^2} + \;\cdot\;\cdot\;\cdot\;\cdot$$

When $\frac{v^2}{c^2}$ is small compared with unity, the third of these terms is always small in comparison with the second, which last is alone considered in classical mechanics. The first term mc^2 does not contain the velocity, and requires no consideration if we are only dealing with the question as to how the energy of a point-mass depends on the velocity.

Before the advent of relativity, physics recognised two conservation laws of fundamental importance, namely, the law of the conservation of energy and the law of the conservation of mass; these two fundamental laws appeared to be quite independent of each other. By means of the theory of relativity they have been united into one law.

The principle of relativity requires that the law of the conservation of energy should hold not only with reference to a co-ordinate system K, but also with respect to every co-ordinate system K' which is in a state of uniform motion of translation relative to K, or, briefly, relative to every "Galileian" system of co-ordinates. In contrast to classical mechanics, the Lorentz transformation is the deciding factor in the transition from one such system to another.

By means of comparatively simple considerations we are led to draw the following conclusion from these premises, in conjunction with the fundamental equations of the electrodynamics of Maxwell: A body moving with the velocity v, which absorbs an amount of energy E_0 in the form of radiation without suffering an alteration in velocity in the process, has, as a consequence, its energy increased by an amount

$$\frac{E_0}{\sqrt{1 - \dfrac{v^2}{c^2}}}$$

In consideration of the expression given above for the kinetic energy of the body, the required energy of the body comes out to be

$$\frac{\left(m + \dfrac{E_0}{c^2}\right)c^2}{\sqrt{1 - \dfrac{v^2}{c^2}}}.$$

Thus the body has the same energy as a body of mass $\left(m + \dfrac{E_0}{c^2}\right)$ moving with the velocity v. Hence we can say: If a body takes up an amount of energy E_0, then its inertial mass increases by an amount $\dfrac{E_0}{c^2}$; the inertial mass of a body is not a constant, but varies according to the change in the energy of the body. The inertial mass of a system of bodies can even be regarded as a measure of its energy. The law of the conservation of the mass of a system becomes identical with the law of the conservation of energy, and is only valid provided that the system neither takes up nor sends out energy. Writing the expression for the energy in the form

$$\frac{mc^2 + E_0}{\sqrt{1 - \dfrac{v^2}{c^2}}},$$

we see that the term mc^2 is nothing else than the energy possessed by the body before it absorbed the energy E_0.

A direct comparison of this relation with experiment is not possible at the present time, owing to the fact that the changes in energy E_0 to which we can subject a system are not large enough to make themselves perceptible as a change in the inertial mass of the system. $\dfrac{E_0}{c^2}$ is too small in comparison with the mass m, which was present before the alteration of the energy. It is owing to this circumstance that classical mechanics was able to establish successfully the conservation of mass as a law of independent validity.

XVI. EXPERIENCE AND THE SPECIAL THEORY OF RELATIVITY

It is known that cathode rays and the so-called β-rays emitted by radioactive substances consist of negatively electrified particles (electrons) of very small inertia and large velocity. By examining the deflection of these rays under the influence of electric and magnetic fields, we can study the law of motion of these particles very exactly.

In the theoretical treatment of these electrons, we are faced with the difficulty that electrodynamic theory of itself is unable to give an account of their nature. For since electrical masses of one sign repel each other, the negative electrical masses constituting the electron would necessarily be scattered under the influence of their mutual repulsions, unless there are forces of another kind operating between them, the nature of which has hitherto remained obscure to us. If we now assume that the relative distances between the electrical masses constituting the electron remain unchanged during the motion of the electron (rigid connection in the sense of classical mechanics), we arrive at a law of motion of the electron which does not agree with experience. Guided by purely formal points of view, H. A. Lorentz was the first to introduce the hypothesis that the particles constituting the electron experience a contraction in the direction of motion in consequence of that motion, the amount of this contraction being proportional to the expression $\sqrt{1 - \dfrac{v^2}{c^2}}$. This hypothesis, which is not justifiable by any electrodynamical facts, supplies us then with that particular law of motion which has been confirmed with great precision in recent years.

The theory of relativity leads to the same law of motion, without requiring any special hypothesis whatsoever as to the structure and the behaviour of the electron.

XVII. MINKOWSKI'S FOUR-DIMENSIONAL SPACE

SPACE is a three-dimensional continuum. By this we mean that it is possible to describe the position of a point (at rest) by means of three numbers (co-ordinates) x, y, z, and that there is an indefinite number of points in the neighbourhood of this one, the position of which can be described by co-ordinates such as x_1, y_1, z_1, which may be as near as we choose to the respective values of the co-ordinates x, y, z of the first point. In virtue of the latter property we speak of a "continuum," and owing to the fact that there are three co-ordinates we speak of it as being "three-dimensional."

Similarly, the world of physical phenomena which was briefly called "world" by Minkowski is naturally four-dimensional in the space-time sense. For it is composed of individual events, each of which is described by four numbers, namely, three space co-ordinates x, y, z and a time co-ordinate, the time-value t. The "world" is in this sense also a continuum; for to every event there are as many "neighbouring" events (realised or at least thinkable) as we care to choose, the co-ordinates x_1, y_1, z_1, t_1 of which differ by an indefinitely small amount from those of the event x, y, z, t originally considered. As a matter of fact, according to classical mechanics, time is absolute, *i.e.* it is independent of the position and the condition of motion of the system of co-ordinates. We see this expressed in the last equation of the Galileian transformation ($t' = t$).

The four-dimensional mode of consideration of the "world" is natural on the theory of relativity, since according to this theory time is robbed of its independence. But the discovery of Minkowski, which was of importance for the formal development of the theory of relativity, does not lie here. It is to be found rather in the fact of his recognition that the four-dimensional space-time continuum of the theory of relativity, in its most essential formal properties, shows a pronounced relationship to the three-dimensional continuum of Euclidean geometrical space. In order to give due prominence to this relationship, however, we must replace the usual time co-ordinate t by an imaginary magnitude $\sqrt{-1}$. ct proportional to it. Under these conditions, the natural laws satisfying the demands of the (special) theory of relativity assume mathematical forms, in which the time co-ordinate plays exactly the same role as the three space co-ordinates. Formally, these four co-ordinates correspond exactly to the three space co-ordinates in Euclidean geometry. It must be clear even to the non-mathematician that, as a consequence of this purely formal addition to our knowledge, the theory perforce gained clearness in no mean measure.

PART TWO: THE GENERAL THEORY OF RELATIVITY

XVIII. SPECIAL AND GENERAL PRINCIPLE OF RELATIVITY

THE BASAL PRINCIPLE, which was the pivot of all our previous considerations, was the *special* principle of relativity, *i.e.* the principle of the physical relativity of all *uniform* motion.

The principle we have made use of not only maintains that we may equally well choose the carriage or the embankment as our reference-body for the description of any event. Our principle rather asserts what follows: If we formulate the general laws of nature as they are obtained from experience, by making use of

(*a*) the embankment as reference-body,

(*b*) the railway carriage as reference-body,

then these general laws of nature (*e.g.* the laws of mechanics or the law of the propagation of light *in vacuo*) have exactly the same form in both cases. This can also be expressed as follows: For the *physical* description of natural processes, neither of the reference-bodies K, K' is unique (lit. "specially marked out") as compared with the other. Unlike the first, this latter statement need not of necessity hold *a priori*; it is not contained in the conceptions of "motion" and "reference-body" and derivable from them; only *experience* can decide as to its correctness or incorrectness.

We started out from the assumption that there exists a reference-body K, whose condition of motion is such that the Galileian law holds with respect to it: A particle left to itself and sufficiently far removed from all other particles moves uniformly in a straight line. With reference to K (Galileian reference-body) the laws of nature were to be as simple as possible. But in addition to K, all bodies of reference K' should be given preference in this sense, and they should be exactly equivalent to K for the formulation of natural laws, provided that they are in a state of *uniform rectilinear and non-rotary motion* with respect to K; all these bodies of reference are to be regarded as Galileian reference-bodies. The validity of the principle of relativity was assumed only for these reference-bodies, but not for others (*e.g.* those possessing motion of a different kind). In this sense we speak of the *special* principle of relativity, or special theory of relativity.

In contrast to this we wish to understand by the "general principle of relativity" the following statement: All bodies of reference K, K', etc., are equivalent for the description of natural phenomena (formulation of the general laws of nature), whatever may be their state of motion.

Let us imagine ourselves transferred to our old friend the railway carriage, which is travelling at a uniform rate. As long as it is moving uniformly, the occupant of the carriage is not sensible of its motion, and it is for this reason that he can without reluctance interpret the facts of the case as indicating that the carriage is at rest, but the embankment in motion. Moreover, according to the special principle of relativity, this interpretation is quite justified also from a physical point of view.

If the motion of the carriage is now changed into a non-uniform motion, as for instance by a powerful application of the brakes, then the occupant of the carriage experiences a correspondingly powerful jerk forwards. It is clear that the Galileian law does not hold with respect to the non-uniformly moving carriage. Because of this, we feel compelled at the present juncture to grant a kind of absolute physical reality to non-uniform motion, in opposition to the general principle of relativity.

XIX. THE GRAVITATIONAL FIELD

"IF WE PICK UP a stone and then let it go, why does it fall to the ground?" The usual answer to this question is: "Because it is attracted by the earth." Modern physics formulates the answer rather differently for the following reason. As a result of the more careful study of electromagnetic phenomena, we have come to regard action at a distance as a process impossible without the intervention of some intermediary medium. If, for instance, a magnet attracts a piece of iron, we cannot be content to regard this as meaning that the magnet acts directly on the iron through the intermediate empty space, but we are constrained to imagine—after the manner of Faraday—that the magnet always calls into being something physically real in the space around it, that something being what we call a "magnetic field." In its turn this magnetic field operates on the piece of iron, so that the latter strives to move towards the magnet.

The action of the earth on the stone takes place indirectly. The earth produces in its surroundings a gravitational field, which acts on the stone and produces its motion of fall. As we know from experience, the intensity of the action on a body diminishes according to a quite definite law, as we proceed farther and farther away from the earth. From our point of view this means: The body (*e.g.* the earth) produces a field in its immediate neighbourhood directly; the intensity and direction of the field at points farther removed from the body are thence determined by the law which governs the properties in space of the gravitational fields themselves.

In contrast to electric and magnetic fields, the gravitational field exhibits a most remarkable property, which is of fundamental importance for what follows. Bodies which are moving under the sole influence of a gravitational field receive an acceleration, *which does not in the least depend either on the material or on the physical state of the body*. This law, which holds most accurately, can be expressed in a different form in the light of the following consideration.

According to Newton's law of motion, we have

$$(\text{Force}) = (\text{inertial mass}) \times (\text{acceleration}),$$

where the "inertial mass" is a characteristic constant of the accelerated body. If now gravitation is the cause of the acceleration, we then have

(Force) = (gravitational mass) $\times$ (intensity of the
gravitational field),

where the "gravitational mass" is likewise a characteristic constant for the body. From these two relations follows:

(acceleration) = $\dfrac{\text{(gravitational mass)}}{\text{(inertial mass)}} \times$ (intensity of the
gravitational field).

If now, as we find from experience, the acceleration is to be independent of the nature and the condition of the body and always the same for a given gravitational field, then the ratio of the gravitational to the inertial mass must likewise be the same for all bodies. By a suitable choice of units we can thus make this ratio equal to unity. We then have the following law: The *gravitational* mass of a body is equal to its *inertial* mass.

It is true that this important law had hitherto been recorded in mechanics, but it had not been *interpreted*. A satisfactory interpretation can be obtained only if we recognise the following fact: *The same* quality of a body manifests itself according to circumstances as "inertia" or as "weight" (lit. "heaviness").

XX. THE EQUALITY OF INERTIAL AND GRAVITATIONAL MASS AS AN ARGUMENT FOR THE GENERAL POSTULATE OF RELATIVITY

We imagine a large portion of empty space, so far removed from stars and other appreciable masses that we have before us approximately the conditions required by the fundamental law of Galilei. As reference-body let us imagine a spacious chest resembling a room with an observer inside who is equipped with apparatus. Gravitation naturally does not exist for this observer. He must fasten himself with strings to the floor, otherwise the slightest impact against the floor will cause him to rise slowly towards the ceiling of the room.

To the middle of the lid of the chest is fixed externally a hook with rope attached, and now a "being" (what kind of a being is immaterial to us) begins pulling at this with a constant force. The chest together with the observer then begins to move "upwards" with a uniformly accelerated motion. In course of time its velocity will reach unheard-of values—provided that we are viewing all this from another reference-body which is not being pulled with a rope.

But how does the man in the chest regard the process? The acceleration of the chest will be transmitted to him by the reaction of the floor of the chest. If he release a body which he previously had in his hand, the acceleration of the chest will no longer be transmitted to this body, and for this reason the body will approach the floor of the chest with an accelerated relative motion. The observer will further convince himself *that the acceleration of the body towards the floor of the chest is always of the same magnitude, whatever kind of body he may happen to use for the experiment.*

Relying on his knowledge of the gravitational field (as it was discussed in the preceding chapter), the man in the chest will thus come to the conclusion that he and the chest are in a gravitational field which is constant with regard to time. Of course he will be puzzled for a moment as to why the chest does not fall in this gravitational field. Just then, however, he discovers the hook in the middle of the lid of the chest and the rope which is attached to it, and he consequently comes to the conclusion that the chest is suspended at rest in the gravitational field.

Even though it is being accelerated with respect to the "Galileian space" first considered, we can nevertheless regard the chest as being at rest. We have thus good grounds for extending the principle of relativity to include bodies of reference which are accelerated with respect to each other, and as a result we have gained a powerful argument for a generalised postulate of relativity.

Suppose that the man in the chest fixes a rope to the inner side of the lid, and that he attaches a body to the free end of the rope. The result of this will be to stretch the rope so that it will hang "vertically" downwards. If we ask for an opinion of the cause of tension in the rope, the man in the chest will say: "The suspended body experiences a downward force in the gravitational field, and this is neutralised by the tension of the rope; what determines the magnitude of the tension of the rope is the *gravitational mass* of the suspended body." On the other hand, an observer who is poised freely in space will interpret the condition of things thus: "The rope must perforce take part in the accelerated motion of the chest, and it transmits this motion to the body attached to it. The tension of the rope is just large enough to effect the acceleration of the body. That which determines the magnitude of the tension of the rope is the *inertial mass* of the body." Guided by this example, we see that our extension of the principle of relativity implies the *necessity* of the law of the equality of inertial and gravitational mass. Thus we have obtained a physical interpretation of this law.

We can now appreciate why that argument is not convincing which we brought forward against the general principle of relativity at the end of Chapter XVIII. It is certainly true that the observer in the railway carriage experiences a jerk forwards as a result of the application of the brake, and that he recognises in this the non-uniformity of motion (retardation) of the carriage. But he is compelled by nobody to refer this jerk to a "real" acceleration (retardation) of the carriage. He might also interpret his experience thus: "My body of reference (the carriage) remains permanently at rest. With reference to it, however, there exists (during the period of application of the brakes) a gravitational field which is directed forwards and which is variable with respect to time. Under the influence of this field, the embankment together with the earth moves non-uniformly in such a manner that their original velocity in the backwards direction is continuously reduced."

XXI. IN WHAT RESPECTS ARE THE FOUNDATIONS OF CLASSICAL MECHANICS AND OF THE SPECIAL THEORY OF RELATIVITY UNSATISFACTORY?

WE HAVE ALREADY STATED several times that classical mechanics starts out from the following law: Material particles sufficiently far removed from other material particles continue to move uniformly in a straight line or continue in a state of rest. We have also repeatedly emphasised that this fundamental law can only be valid for bodies of reference K which possess certain unique states of motion, and which are in uniform translational motion relative to each other. Relative to other reference-bodies K the law is not valid. Both in classical mechanics and in the special theory of relativity we therefore differentiate between reference-bodies K relative to which the recognised "laws of nature" can be said to hold and reference-bodies K relative to which these laws do not hold.

But no person whose mode of thought is logical can rest satisfied with this condition of things. He asks: "How does it come that certain reference-bodies (or their states of motion) are given priority over other reference-bodies (or their states of motion)? *What is the reason for this preference?*"

I seek in vain for a real something in classical mechanics (or in the special theory of relativity) to which I can attribute the different behaviour of bodies considered with respect to the reference-systems K and K'. Newton saw this objection and attempted to invalidate it, but without success. It can only be got rid of by means of a physics which is conformable to the general principle of relativity, since the equations of such a theory hold for every body of reference, whatever may be its state of motion.

XXII. A FEW INFERENCES FROM THE GENERAL THEORY OF RELATIVITY

THE CONSIDERATIONS of Chapter XX show that the general theory of relativity puts us in a position to derive properties of the gravitational field in a purely theoretical manner. Let us suppose, for instance, that we know the space-time "course" for any natural process whatsoever, as regards the manner in which it takes place in the Galileian domain relative to a Galileian body of reference K. By means of purely theoretical operations (*i.e.* simply by calculation) we are then able to find how this known natural process appears, as seen from a reference-body K' which is accelerated relatively to K. But since a gravitational field exists with respect to this new body of reference K', our consideration also teaches us how the gravitational field influences the process studied.

For example, we learn that a body which is in a state of uniform rectilinear motion with respect to K (in accordance with the law of Galilei) is executing an accelerated and in general curvilinear motion with respect to the accelerated reference-body K' (chest). This acceleration or curvature corresponds to the influence on the moving body of the gravitational field prevailing relatively to K'. It is known that a gravitational field influences the movement of bodies in this way, so that our consideration supplies us with nothing essentially new.

However, we obtain a new result of fundamental importance when we carry out the analogous consideration for a ray of light. With respect to the Galileian reference-body K, such a ray of light is transmitted rectilinearly with the velocity c. It can easily be shown that the path of the same ray of light is no longer a straight line when we consider it with reference to the accelerated chest (reference-body K'). From this we conclude *that, in general, rays of light are propagated curvilinearly in gravitational fields.*

Although a detailed examination of the question shows that the curvature of light rays required by the general theory of relativity is only exceedingly small for the gravitational fields at our disposal in practice, its estimated magnitude for light rays passing the sun at grazing incidence is nevertheless 1.7 seconds of arc. This ought to manifest itself in the following way: As seen from the earth, certain fixed stars appear to be in the neighbourhood of the sun, and are thus capable of observation during a total eclipse of the sun. At such times, these stars ought to appear to be displaced outwards from the sun by an amount indicated above, as compared with their apparent position in the sky when the sun is situated at another part of the heavens. The examination of the correctness or otherwise of this deduction is a problem of the greatest importance, the early solution of which is to be expected of astronomers.[1]

In the second place our result shows that, according to the general theory of relativity, the law of the constancy of the velocity of light *in vacuo*, which constitutes one of the two fundamental assumptions in the special theory of relativity and to which we have already frequently referred, cannot claim any unlimited validity. A curvature of rays of light can only take place when the velocity of propagation of light varies with position. Now we might think that as a consequence of this, the special theory of relativity and with it the whole theory of relativity would be laid in the dust. But in reality this is not the case. We can only conclude that the special theory of relativity cannot claim an unlimited domain of validity; its results hold only so long as we are able to disregard the influences of gravitational fields on the phenomena (*e.g.* of light).

[1]By means of the star photographs of two expeditions equipped by a Joint Committee of the Royal and Royal Astronomical Societies, the existence of the deflection of light demanded by theory was confirmed during the solar eclipse of May 29, 1919.

The most attractive problem, to the solution of which the general theory of relativity supplies the key, concerns the investigation of the laws satisfied by the gravitational field itself. Let us consider this for a moment.

We are acquainted with space-time domains which behave (approximately) in a "Galileian" fashion under suitable choice of reference-body, *i.e.* domains in which gravitational fields are absent. If we now refer such a domain to a reference-body K' possessing any kind of motion, then relative to K' there exists a gravitational field which is variable with respect to space and time. According to the general theory of relativity, the general law of the gravitational field must be satisfied for all gravitational fields obtainable in this way.

XXIII. BEHAVIOUR OF CLOCKS AND MEASURING RODS ON A ROTATING BODY OF REFERENCE

WE START OFF AGAIN from quite special cases, which we have frequently used before. Let us consider a space-time domain in which no gravitational field exists relative to a reference-body K whose state of motion has been suitably chosen. K is then a Galileian reference-body as regards the domain considered, and the results of the special theory of relativity hold relative to K. Let us suppose the same domain referred to a second body of reference K', which is rotating uniformly with respect to K. In order to fix our ideas, we shall imagine K' to be in the form of a plane circular disc, which rotates uniformly in its own plane about its centre. An observer who is sitting eccentrically on the disc K' is sensible of a force which acts outwards in a radial direction, and which would be interpreted as an effect of inertia (centrifugal force) by an observer who was at rest with respect to the original reference-body K. But the observer on the disc may regard his disc as a reference-body which is "at rest." The force acting on himself, and in fact on all other bodies which are at rest relative to the disc, he regards as the effect of a gravitational field.

The observer performs experiments on his circular disc with clocks and measuring rods. In doing so, it is his intention to arrive at exact definitions for the signification of time- and space-data with reference to the circular disc K', these definitions being based on his observations.

To start with, he places one of two identically constructed clocks at the centre of the circular disc, and the other on the edge of the disc, so that they are at rest relative to it. As judged from this body, the clock at the centre of the disc has no velocity, whereas the clock at the edge of the disc is in motion relative to K in consequence of the rotation. According to a result obtained in Chapter XII, it follows that the latter clock goes at a rate permanently slower than that of the clock at the centre of the circular disc, *i.e.* as observed from K. Thus on our circular disc, or, to make the case more general, in every gravitational field, a clock will go more quickly or less quickly, according to the position in which the clock is situated (at rest). For this reason it is not possible to obtain a reasonable definition of time with the aid of clocks which are arranged at rest with respect to the body of reference.

If the observer applies his standard measuring rod (a rod which is short as compared with the radius of the disc) tangentially to the edge of the disc, then, as judged from the Galileian system, the length of this rod will be less than 1, since, according to Chapter XII, moving bodies suffer a shortening in the direction of the motion. On the other hand, the measuring rod will not experience a shortening in length, as judged from *K*, if it is applied to the disc in the direction of the radius. If, then, the observer first measures the circumference of the disc with his measuring rod and then the diameter of the disc, on dividing the one by the other, he will not obtain as quotient the familiar number $\pi = 3.14 \ldots$, but a larger number, whereas of course, for a disc which is at rest with respect to *K*, this operation would yield π exactly. This proves that the propositions of Euclidean geometry cannot hold exactly on the rotating disc, nor in general in a gravitational field, at least if we attribute the length 1 to the rod in all positions and in every orientation. Hence the idea of a straight line also loses its meaning. We are therefore not in a position to define exactly the co-ordinates *x, y, z* relative to the disc by means of the method used in discussing the special theory, and as long as the co-ordinates and times of events have not been defined we cannot assign an exact meaning to the natural laws in which these occur.

XXIV. EUCLIDEAN AND NON-EUCLIDEAN CONTINUUM

THE SURFACE of a marble table is spread out in front of me. I can get from any one point on this table to any other point by passing continuously from one point to a "neighbouring" one, and repeating this process a (large) number of times, or, in other words, by going from point to point without executing "jumps." We express this property of the surface by describing the latter as a continuum.

Let us now imagine that a large number of little rods of equal length have been made, their lengths being small compared with the dimensions of the marble slab. We next lay four of these little rods on the marble slab so that they constitute a quadrilateral figure (a square), the diagonals of which are equally long. To this square we add similar ones, each of which has one rod in common with the first. We proceed in like manner with each of these squares until finally the whole marble slab is laid out with squares.

If everything has really gone smoothly, then I say that the points of the marble slab constitute a Euclidean continuum with respect to the little rod, which has been used as a "distance" (line-interval). By choosing one corner of a square as "origin," I can characterise every other corner of a square with reference to this origin by means of two numbers. I only need state how many rods I must pass over when, starting from the origin, I proceed towards the "right" and then "upwards," in order to arrive at the corner of the square under consideration. These two numbers are then the "Cartesian co-ordinates" of this corner with reference to the "Cartesian co-ordinate system" which is determined by the arrangement of little rods.

We recognise that there must also be cases in which the experiment would be unsuccessful. We shall suppose that the rods "expand" by an amount proportional to the increase of temperature. We heat the central part of the marble slab, but not the periphery, in which case two of our little rods can still be brought into coincidence at every position on the table. But our construction of squares must necessarily come into disorder during the heating, because the little rods on the central region of the table expand, whereas those on the outer part do not.

With reference to our little rods—defined as unit lengths—the marble slab is no longer a Euclidean continuum, and we are also no longer in the position of defining Cartesian co-ordinates directly with their aid, since the above construction can no longer be carried out.

If rods of every kind (*i.e.* of every material) were to behave *in the same way* as regards the influence of temperature when they are on the variably heated marble slab, and if we had no other means of detecting the effect of temperature than the geometrical behaviour of our rods in experiments analogous to the one described here, then our best plan would be to assign the distance *one* to two points on the slab, provided that the ends of one of our rods could be made to coincide with these two points.

The method of Cartesian co-ordinates must then be discarded, and replaced by another which does not assume the validity of Euclidean geometry for rigid bodies. The reader will notice that the situation depicted here corresponds to the one brought about by the general postulate of relativity.

XXV. GAUSSIAN CO-ORDINATES

According to Gauss, this combined analytical and geometrical mode of handling the problem can be arrived at in the following way. We imagine a system of arbitrary curves (see Fig. 4) drawn on the surface of the table. These we designate as u-curves, and we indicate each of them by means of a number. The curves $u = 1$, $u = 2$, and $u = 3$ are drawn in the diagram. Between the curves $u = 1$ and $u = 2$ we must imagine an infinitely large number to be drawn, all of which correspond to real numbers lying between 1 and 2. We have then a system of u-curves, and this "infinitely dense" system covers the whole surface of the table. These u-curves must not intersect each other, and through each point of the surface one and only one curve must pass. Thus a perfectly definite value of u belongs to every point on the surface of the marble slab. In like manner we imagine a system of v-curves drawn on the surface. These satisfy the same conditions as the *u*-curves, they are provided with numbers in a corresponding manner, and they may likewise be of arbitrary shape. It follows that a value of *u* and a value of *v* belong to every point on the surface of the table. For example, the point *P* in the diagram has the

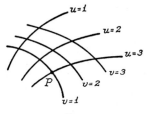

FIG. 4.

Gaussian co-ordinates $u = 3$, $v = 1$. Two neighbouring points *P* and *P'* on the surface then correspond to the co-ordinates

P:	u, v
P':	$u + du, v + dv,$

where *du* and *dv* signify very small numbers. In a similar manner we may indicate the distance (line-interval) between *P* and *P'*, as measured with a little rod, by means of the ·very small number *ds*. Then according to Gauss we have

$$ds^2 = g_{11} \ du^2 + 2g_{12} \ du \ dv + g_{22} \ dv^2,$$

where g_{11}, g_{12}, g_{22} are magnitudes which depend in a perfectly definite way on *u* and *v*. The magnitudes g_{11}, g_{12}, and g_{22} determine the behaviour of the rods relative to the *u*-curves and *v*-curves, and thus also relative to the surface of the table.

For the case in which the points of the surface considered form a Euclidean continuum with reference to the measuring rods, but only in this case, it is possible to draw the *u*-curves and *v*-curves and to attach numbers to them, in such a manner, that we simply have:

$$ds^2 = du^2 + dv^2.$$

Under these conditions, the *u*-curves and *v*-curves are straight lines in the sense of Euclidean geometry, and they are perpendicular to each other. Here the Gaussian co-ordinates are simply Cartesian ones. It is clear that Gauss co-ordinates are nothing more than an association of two sets of numbers with the points of the surface considered, of such a nature that numerical values differing very slightly from each other are associated with neighbouring points "in space."

So far, these considerations hold for a continuum of two dimensions. But the Gaussian method can be applied also to a continuum of three, four, or more dimensions. If, for instance, a continuum of four dimensions be supposed available, we may represent it in the following way. With every point of the continuum we associate arbitrarily four numbers,

x_1, x_2, x_3, x_4, which are known as "co-ordinates." Adjacent points correspond to adjacent values of the co-ordinates. If a distance ds is associated with the adjacent points P and P', this distance being measurable and well-defined from a physical point of view, then the following formula holds:

$$ds^2 = g_{11}\, dx_1{}^2 + 2g_{12}\, dx_1\, dx_2 \cdot \cdot \cdot \cdot + g_{44}\, dx_4{}^2,$$

where the magnitudes g_{11}, etc., have values which vary with the position in the continuum.

We can sum this up as follows: Gauss invented a method for the mathematical treatment of continua in general, in which "size-relations" ("distances" between neighbouring points) are defined. To every point of a continuum are assigned as many numbers (Gaussian co-ordinates) as the continuum has dimensions. This is done in such a way that only one meaning can be attached to the assignment and that numbers (Gaussian co-ordinates) which differ by an indefinitely small amount are assigned to adjacent points. The Gaussian co-ordinate system is a logical generalisation of the Cartesian co-ordinate system. It is also applicable to non-Euclidean continua, but only when, with respect to the defined "size" or "distance," small parts of the continuum under consideration behave more nearly like a Euclidean system, the smaller the part of the continuum under our notice.

XXVI. THE SPACE-TIME CONTINUUM OF THE SPECIAL THEORY OF RELATIVITY CONSIDERED AS A EUCLIDEAN CONTINUUM

FOR THE TRANSITION from one Galileian system to another, which is moving uniformly with reference to the first, the equations of the Lorentz transformation are valid. These last form the basis for the derivation of deductions from the special theory of relativity, and in themselves they are nothing more than the expression of the universal validity of the law of transmission of light for all Galileian systems of reference.

Minkowski found that the Lorentz transformations satisfy the following simple conditions. Let us consider two neighbouring events, the relative position of which in the four-dimensional continuum is given with respect to a Galileian reference-body K by the space co-ordinate differences dx, dy, dz and the time-difference dt. With reference to a second Galileian system we shall suppose that the corresponding differences for these two events are dx', dy', dz', dt'. The magnitude

$$ds^2 = dx^2 + dy^2 + dz^2 - c^2\, dt^2,$$

which belongs to two adjacent points of the four-dimensional space-time continuum, has the same value for all selected (Galileian) reference-bodies. If we replace x, y, z, $\sqrt{-1}\, ct$, by x_1, x_2, x_3, x_4, we also obtain the result that

$$ds^2 = dx_1{}^2 + dx_2{}^2 + dx_3{}^2 + dx_4{}^2$$

is independent of the choice of the body of reference. We call the magnitude ds the "distance" apart of the two events or four-dimensional points.

Thus, if we choose as time-variable the imaginary variable $\sqrt{-1}\ ct$ instead of the real quantity t, we can regard the space-time continuum—in accordance with the special theory of relativity—as a "Euclidean" four-dimensional continuum.

XXVII. THE SPACE-TIME CONTINUUM OF THE GENERAL THEORY OF RELATIVITY IS NOT A EUCLIDEAN CONTINUUM

IN THE FIRST PART of this book we were able to make use of space-time co-ordinates which allowed of a simple and direct physical interpretation, and which, according to Chapter XXVI, can be regarded as four-dimensional Cartesian co-ordinates. This was possible on the basis of the law of the constancy of the velocity of light. But according to Chapter XXI, the general theory of relativity cannot retain this law. On the contrary, we arrived at the result that according to this latter theory the velocity of light must always depend on the co-ordinates when a gravitational field is present. In connection with a specific illustration in Chapter XXIII, we found that the presence of a gravitational field invalidates the definition of the co-ordinates and the time, which led us to our objective in the special theory of relativity.

We are led to the conviction that, according to the general principle of relativity, the space-time continuum cannot be regarded as a Euclidean one, but that here we have the general case, corresponding to the marble slab with local variations of temperature. Just as it was there impossible to construct a Cartesian co-ordinate system from equal rods, so here it is impossible to build up a system (reference-body) from rigid bodies and clocks, which shall be of such a nature that measuring rods and clocks, arranged rigidly with respect to one another, shall indicate position and time directly.

But the considerations of Chapter XXV and XXVI show us the way to surmount this difficulty. We refer the four-dimensional space-time continuum in an arbitrary manner to Gauss co-ordinates. We assign to every point of the continuum (event) four numbers, x_1, x_2, x_3, x_4 (co-ordinates), which have not the least direct physical significance, but only serve the purpose of numbering the points of the continuum in a definite but arbitrary manner. This arrangement does not even need to be of such a kind that we must regard x_1, x_2, x_3 as "space" co-ordinates and x_4 as a "time" co-ordinate.

The only statements having regard to these points which can claim a physical existence are in reality the statements about their encounters. In our mathematical treatment, such an encounter is expressed in the fact that the two lines which represent the motions of the points in question have a particular system of co-ordinate values, x_1, x_2, x_3, x_4, in common.

After mature consideration the reader will doubtless admit that in reality such encounters constitute the only actual evidence of a time-space nature with which we meet in physical statements.

The following statements hold generally: Every physical description resolves itself into a number of statements, each of which refers to the space-time coincidence of two events A and B. In terms of Gaussian co-ordinates, every such statement is expressed by the agreement of their four co-ordinates x_1, x_2, x_3, x_4. Thus, in reality, the description of the time-space continuum by means of Gauss co-ordinates completely replaces the description with the aid of a body of reference, without suffering from the defects of the latter mode of description; it is not tied down to the Euclidean character of the continuum which has to be represented.

XXVIII. EXACT FORMULATION OF THE GENERAL PRINCIPLE OF RELATIVITY

THE FOLLOWING STATEMENT corresponds to the fundamental idea of the general principle of relativity: *"All Gaussian co-ordinate systems are essentially equivalent for the formulation of the general laws of nature."*

If we desire to adhere to our "old-time" three-dimensional view of things, then we can characterise the development which is being undergone by the fundamental idea of the general theory of relativity as follows: The special theory of relativity has reference to Galileian domains, *i.e.* to those in which no gravitational field exists. In this connection a Galileian reference-body serves as body of reference, *i.e.* a rigid body the state of motion of which is so chosen that the Galileian law of the uniform rectilinear motion of "isolated" material points holds relatively to it.

In gravitational fields there are no such things as rigid bodies with Euclidean properties; thus the fictitious rigid body of reference is of no avail in the general theory of relativity. The motion of clocks is also influenced by gravitational fields, and in such a way that a physical definition of time which is made directly with the aid of clocks has by no means the same degree of plausibility as in the special theory of relativity.

For this reason non-rigid reference-bodies are used which are as a whole not only moving in any way whatsoever, but which also suffer alterations in form *ad lib.* during their motion. Clocks, for which the law of motion is of any kind, however irregular, serve for the definition of time. We have to imagine each of these clocks fixed at a point on the non-rigid reference-body. These clocks satisfy only the one condition, that the "readings" which are observed simultaneously on adjacent clocks (in space) differ from each other by an indefinitely small amount. This non-rigid reference-body, which might appropriately be termed a "reference-mollusk," is in the main equivalent to a Gaussian four-dimensional co-ordinate system chosen arbitrarily. Every point on the mollusk is treated as a space-point, and every material point which is at rest relatively to it as at rest, so long as the mollusk is considered as reference-body. The general principle of relativity requires that all these mollusks can be used as reference-bodies with equal right and equal success in the formulation of the general laws of nature; the laws themselves must be quite independent of the choice of mollusk.

The great power possessed by the general principle of relativity lies in the comprehensive limitation which is imposed on the laws of nature in consequence of what we have seen above.

XXIX. THE SOLUTION OF THE PROBLEM OF GRAVITATION ON THE BASIS OF THE GENERAL PRINCIPLE OF RELATIVITY

FINALLY, the general principle of relativity permits us to determine the influence of the gravitational field on the course of all those processes which take place according to known laws when a gravitational field is absent, *i.e.* which have already been fitted into the frame of the special theory of relativity; it has also already explained a result of observation in astronomy, against which classical mechanics is powerless. According to Newton's theory, a planet moves round the sun in an ellipse, which would permanently maintain its position with respect to the fixed stars, if we could disregard the motion of the fixed stars themselves and the action of the other planets under consideration. Thus, if we correct the observed motion of the planets for these two influences, and if Newton's theory be strictly correct, we ought to obtain for the orbit of the planet an ellipse, which is fixed with reference to the fixed stars. This deduction, which can be tested with great accuracy, has been confirmed for all the planets save one. The sole exception is Mercury, the planet which lies nearest the sun. Since the time of Leverrier, it has been known that the ellipse corresponding to the orbit of Mercury, after it has been corrected for the influences mentioned above, is not stationary with respect to the fixed stars, but that it rotates exceedingly slowly in the plane of the orbit and in the sense of the orbital motion. The value obtained for this rotary movement of the orbital ellipse was 43 seconds of arc per century, an amount ensured to be correct to within a few seconds of arc. This effect can be explained by means of classical mechanics only on the assumption of hypotheses which have little probability and which were devised solely for this purpose.

On the basis of the general theory of relativity, it is found that the ellipse of every planet round the sun must necessarily rotate in the manner indicated above; that for all the planets, with the exception of Mercury, this rotation is too small to be detected with the delicacy of observation possible at the present time; but that in the case of Mercury it must amount to 43 seconds of arc per century, a result which is strictly in agreement with observation.

Apart from this one, it has hitherto been possible to make only two deductions from the theory which admit of being tested by observation, to wit, the curvature of light rays by the gravitational field of the sun, and a displacement of the spectral lines of light reaching us from large stars, as compared with the corresponding lines for light produced in an analogous manner terrestrially (*i.e.* by the same kind of molecule).

PART THREE: CONSIDERATIONS ON THE UNIVERSE AS A WHOLE

XXX. COSMOLOGICAL DIFFICULTIES OF NEWTON'S THEORY

IF WE PONDER over the question as to how the universe, considered as a whole, is to be regarded, the first answer that suggests itself to us is surely this: As regards space (and time) the universe is infinite. There are stars everywhere, so that the density of matter, although very variable in detail, is nevertheless on the average everywhere the same.

This view is not in harmony with the theory of Newton. The latter theory rather requires that the universe should have a kind of centre in which the density of the stars is a maximum, and that as we proceed outwards from this centre the group-density of the stars should diminish, until finally, at great distances, it is succeeded by an infinite region of emptiness. The stellar universe ought to be a finite island in the infinite ocean of space.

This conception is in itself not very satisfactory. It is still less satisfactory because it leads to the result that the light emitted by the stars and also individual stars of the stellar system are perpetually passing out into infinite space, never to return, and without ever again coming into interaction with other objects of nature. Such a finite material universe would be destined to become gradually but systematically impoverished.

In order to escape this dilemma, Seeliger suggested a modification of Newton's law, in which he assumes that for great distances the force of attraction between two masses diminishes more rapidly than would result from the inverse-square law. In this way it is possible for the mean density of matter to be constant everywhere, even to infinity, without infinitely large gravitational fields being produced.

XXXI. THE POSSIBILITY OF A "FINITE" AND YET "UNBOUNDED" UNIVERSE

BUT SPECULATIONS on the structure of the universe also move in quite another direction. The development of non-Euclidean geometry led to the recognition of the fact that we can cast doubt on the *infiniteness* of our space without coming into conflict with the laws of thought or with experience (Riemann, Helmholtz).

In the first place, we imagine an existence in two-dimensional space.

Flat beings with flat implements, and in particular flat rigid measuring rods, are free to move in a *plane*. For them nothing exists outside of this plane: that which they observe to happen to themselves and to their flat "things" is the all-inclusive reality of their plane. In particular, the constructions of plane Euclidean geometry can be carried out by means of the rods, *e.g.* the lattice construction, considered in Chapter XXIV. In contrast to ours, the universe of these beings is two-dimensional; but, like ours, it extends to infinity. In their universe there is room for an infinite number of identical squares made up of rods, *i.e.* its volume (surface) is infinite. If these beings say their universe is "plane," there is sense in the statement, because they mean that they can perform the constructions of plane Euclidean geometry with their rods. In this connection the individual rods always represent the same distance, independently of their position.

Let us consider now a second two-dimensional existence, but this time on a spherical surface instead of on a plane. The flat beings with their measuring rods and other objects fit exactly on this surface and they are unable to leave it. Their whole universe of observation extends exclusively over the surface of the sphere. Are these beings able to regard the geometry of their universe as being plane geometry and their rods withal as the realisation of "distance"? They cannot do this. For if they attempt to realise a straight line, they will obtain a curve, which we "three-dimensional beings" designate as a great circle, *i.e.* a self-contained line of definite finite length, which can be measured up by means of a measuring rod. Similarly, this universe has a finite area that can be compared with the area of a square constructed with rods. The great charm resulting from this consideration lies in the recognition of the fact that *the universe of these beings is finite and yet has no limits.*

But the spherical-surface beings do not need to go on a world tour in order to perceive that they are not living in a Euclidean universe. They can convince themselves of this on every part of their "world," provided they do not use too small a piece of it. Starting from a point, they draw "straight lines" (arcs of circles as judged in three-dimensional space) of equal length in all directions. They will call the line joining the free ends of these lines a "circle." For a plane surface, the ratio of the circumference of a circle to its diameter, both lengths being measured with the same rod, is, according to Euclidean geometry of the plane, equal to a constant value π, which is independent of the diameter of the circle. On their spherical surface our flat beings would find for this ratio the value

$$\pi \frac{\sin\left(\dfrac{r}{R}\right)}{\left(\dfrac{r}{R}\right)},$$

i.e. a smaller value than π, the difference being the more considerable, the greater is the radius of the circle in comparison with the radius R of the "world-sphere." By means of this relation the spherical beings can determine the radius of their universe ("world"), even when only a relatively small part of their world-sphere is available for their measurements.

Thus if the spherical-surface beings are living on a planet of which the solar system occupies only a negligibly small part of the spherical universe, they have no means of determining whether they are living in a finite or in an infinite universe, because the "piece of universe" to which they have access is in both cases practically plane, or Euclidean. It follows directly from this discussion that for our sphere-beings the circumference of a circle first increases with the radius until the "circumference of the universe" is reached, and that it thenceforward gradually decreases to zero for still further increasing values of the radius. During this process the area of the circle continues to increase more and more, until finally it becomes equal to the total area of the whole "world-sphere."

Perhaps the reader will wonder why we have placed our "beings" on a sphere rather than on another closed surface. But this choice has its justification in the fact that, of all closed surfaces, the sphere is unique in possessing the property that all points on it are equivalent. I admit that the ratio of the circumference c of a circle to its radius r depends on r, but for a given value of r it is the same for all points of the "world-sphere"; in other words, the "world-sphere" is a "surface of constant curvature."

To this two-dimensional sphere-universe there is a three-dimensional analogy, namely, the three-dimensional spherical space which was discovered by Riemann. Its points are likewise all equivalent. It possesses a finite volume, which is determined by its "radius" $(2\pi^2R^3)$.

Suppose we draw lines or stretch strings in all directions from a point, and mark off from each of these the distance r with a measuring rod. All the free end-points of these lengths lie on a spherical surface. We can specially measure up the area (F) of this surface by means of a square made up of measuring rods. If the universe is Euclidean, then $F = 4\pi r^2$; if it is spherical, then F is always less than $4\pi r^2$. With increasing values of r, F increases from zero up to a maximum value which is determined by the "world-radius," but for still further increasing values of r, the area gradually diminishes to zero. At first the straight lines which radiate from the starting point diverge farther and farther from one another, but later they approach each other, and finally they run together again at a "counter-point" to the starting point. Under such conditions they have traversed the whole spherical space. It is easily seen that the three-dimensional spherical space is quite analogous to the two-dimensional spherical surface. It is finite (*i.e.* of finite volume), and has no bounds.

It follows, from what has been said, that closed spaces without limits are conceivable. From amongst these, the spherical space (and the elliptical) excels in its simplicity, since all points on it are equivalent. As a result of this discussion, a most interesting question arises for astronomers and physicists, and that is whether the universe in which we live is infinite or whether it is finite in the manner of the spherical universe. Our experience is far from being sufficient to enable us to answer this question. But the general theory of relativity permits of our answering it with a moderate degree of certainty.

XXXII. THE STRUCTURE OF SPACE ACCORDING TO THE GENERAL THEORY OF RELATIVITY

ACCORDING TO the general theory of relativity, the geometrical properties of space are not independent, but they are determined by matter. Thus we can draw conclusions about the geometrical structure of the universe only if we base our considerations on the state of the matter as being something that is known. We know from experience that, for a suitably chosen co-ordinate system, the velocities of the stars are small as compared with the velocity of transmission of light. We can thus as a rough approximation arrive at a conclusion as to the nature of the universe as a whole, if we treat the matter as being at rest.

We already know from our previous discussion that the behaviour of measuring rods and clocks is influenced by gravitational fields, *i.e.* by the distribution of matter. This in itself is sufficient to exclude the possibility of the exact validity of Euclidean geometry in our universe. But it is conceivable that our universe differs only slightly from a Euclidean one, and this notion seems all the more probable, since calculations show that the metrics of surrounding space is influenced only to an exceedingly small extent by masses even of the magnitude of our sun. We might imagine that, as regards geometry, our universe behaves analogously to a surface which is irregularly curved in its individual parts, but which nowhere departs appreciably from a plane: something like the rippled surface of a lake. Such a universe might fittingly be called a quasi-Euclidean universe. As regards its space it would be infinite. But calculation shows that in a quasi-Euclidean universe the average density of matter would necessarily be *nil*. Thus such a universe could not be inhabited by matter everywhere; it would present to us that unsatisfactory picture which we portrayed in Chapter XXX.

If we are to have in the universe an average density of matter which differs from zero, however small may be that difference, then the universe cannot be quasi-Euclidean. On the contrary, the results of calculation indicate that if matter be distributed uniformly, the universe would necessarily be spherical (or elliptical). Since in reality the detailed distribution of matter is not uniform, the real universe will deviate in individual parts from the spherical, *i.e.* the universe will be quasi-spherical. But it will be necessarily finite. In fact, the theory supplies us with a simple connection between the space-expanse of the universe and the average density of matter in it.

Catalog

If you are interested in a list of fine Paperback
books, covering a wide range of subjects
and interests, send your name and address,
requesting your free catalog, to:

McGraw-Hill Paperbacks
1221 Avenue of Americas
New York, N.Y. 10020